Rivers

of

REVELATION

Rivers
of
REVELATION

RABBI KIRT A. SCHNEIDER

CHARISMA HOUSE

Most CHARISMA HOUSE BOOK GROUP products are available at special quantity discounts for bulk purchase for sales promotions, premiums, fund-raising, and educational needs. For details, write Charisma House Book Group, 600 Rinehart Road, Lake Mary, Florida 32746, or telephone (407) 333-0600.

RIVERS OF REVELATION by Rabbi Kirt A. Schneider
Published by Charisma House
Charisma Media/Charisma House Book Group
600 Rinehart Road
Lake Mary, Florida 32746
www.charismahouse.com

Visit the author's website at https://discoveringthejewishjesus.com.

Library of Congress Cataloging-in-Publication Data

Names: Schneider, K. A. (Kirt Allan), author.
Title: Rivers of revelation / by Rabbi Kirt A. Schneider.
Description: Lake Mary, Florida : Charisma House, [2019]
Identifiers: LCCN 2019029547 (print) | LCCN 2019029548 (ebook) |
ISBN
   9781629996516 (hardcover) | ISBN 9781629996523 (ebook)
Subjects: LCSH: Revelation--Biblical teaching. | Revelation--
Meditations. |
   Messianic Judaism.
Classification: LCC BT126 .S36 2019 (print) | LCC BT126 (ebook) |
DDC
   231.7/4--dc23
LC record available at https://lccn.loc.gov/2019029547
LC ebook record available at https://lccn.loc.gov/2019029548

19 20 21 22 23 — 987654321
Printed in the United States of America

Contents

Acknowledgments

To a degree we are all products of those around us who have invested into our lives. God often uses others to impart something of Himself to us. With this in mind, I want to thank my wife, Cynthia, and it goes without saying, Baruch HaShem; I thank the Lord.

Introduction

REVELATION RECEIVED FROM the Spirit of God always changes lives. You see, true faith is built on revelation because revelation shows us who God is, who we are in Him, and the authority we have been given as the children of God.

We see this in Matthew 16 when Jesus asked His disciples, "Who do you say that I am?" (v. 15).

> Simon Peter answered, "You are the Christ, the Son of the living God." And Jesus said to him, "Blessed are you, Simon Barjona, because flesh and blood did not reveal this to you, but My Father who is in heaven. I also say to you that you are Peter, and upon this rock I will build My church; and the gates of Hades will not overpower it. I will give you the keys of the kingdom of heaven; and whatever you bind on earth shall have been bound in heaven, and whatever you loose on earth shall have been loosed in heaven."
> —MATTHEW 16:16–19

In this account God revealed to Peter not only who Jesus was—"the Christ, the Son of the living God"—but also who Peter himself was and the authority God was giving to the church so that we could make Him known in the earth.

Revelation is supernatural, and it is always transformational. This is why the Bible tells us in Ephesians 1:17 to pray "that the God of our Lord Jesus Christ, the Father of glory, may give to [us] a spirit of wisdom and of revelation in the knowledge of Him."

My prayer is that as you journey through the next one hundred days God will give you a spirit of Wisdom and Revelation. I wrote these devotionals in hope that the Father would use them to reveal His truth to you in a fresh way so that you can walk in the fullness of who God has called you to be and become a bold witness for Him in the earth.

I called this book *Rivers of Revelation* because I believe that as you drink of God's Word, out of your innermost being will flow rivers of living water. You will come to know God in a deeper way, and the revelation you glean will flow from you out to others as you share the truth.

Please don't rush through these pages. Allow the Holy Spirit to speak to your heart through these pearls of truth. Pray as you read each one, and write down any additional insights the Holy Spirit gives you.

Through revelation we walk in power. Through revelation we are changed.

> Beloved, now we are children of God; and it has not yet been revealed what we shall be, but we know that when He is revealed, we shall be like Him, for we shall see Him as He is.
>
> —1 John 3:2

You Too Have Been Chosen

He chose us in Him before the foundation of the world, that we would be holy and blameless before Him. In love He predestined us to adoption as sons through Jesus Christ to Himself, according to the kind intention of His will.

—EPHESIANS 1:4–5

ONE OF THE most foundational truths that has anchored me in God is the realization that I have been chosen. As a new believer in 1978, I looked around and wondered why I was the only Jewish person in my whole school, which had many Jews, who believed in Jesus. Then I realized that I believed because God had revealed Himself to me in a way that He had not revealed Himself to the other Jewish people in my school. I realized He had chosen me.

In John 17 Jesus prayed for those whom the Father had given Him. And in John 6 Jesus said that no one can come to Him unless it had been granted from the Father and that all whom the Father had given Him would come to Him (vv. 65, 37).

Beloved, it is an awesome blessing when you realize that you were personally and specifically chosen by God the Father before the foundation of the world. And because He chose you, He revealed Jesus to you, gave you faith, and brought you to Himself. Even if your coming to faith wasn't dramatic but happened slowly over time, you came to faith by the supernatural work of the Holy Spirit because the Father had chosen you even before you were born.

When you realize that the security of your relationship with the Father is based on His choice of you, you will know that you are standing on solid ground. Jesus said in John 15, "You did not choose Me but I chose you" (v. 16). Taking a hold of this truth will give you a confidence in your relationship with God that can come no other way.

> *Father God, in Messiah Jesus' name I ask You to open the eyes of my understanding to be able to realize that truly You chose me before the foundation of the world because You love me. Because my relationship with You is rooted in Your choice of me and Your love for me will never change, I can be secure in You. Help me to take hold of this.*

Be Still

Be still, and know that I am God; I will be exalted
among the nations, I will be exalted in the earth!
—Psalm 46:10, nkjv

THE HOLY SPIRIT is alive, and He is moving within us. But we can become so involved in our own efforts that we miss what the Holy Spirit is doing. This is why the Lord tells us in Psalm 46:10 to be still and know that He is God. Or as the New American Standard Bible puts it, we are to "cease striving" and know that He is God.

I believe peace precedes power and authority. When we are still, we are able to enter into the peace of God, and the peace of God produces the fruit of God's Spirit. Many times in Scripture the Lord is referred to as the God of peace. And Romans 16:20 tells us that "the God of peace will soon crush Satan under [our] feet." The God of peace is a mighty warrior, and by resting in His peace, by ceasing our striving, we obtain victory.

I want to encourage you, beloved one, with a very practical suggestion: take time to be still before God.

You can do this anytime—sitting on your couch at home or even while you're driving in your car. Silence your phone, turn off the radio, and just be still before God. You may feel that nothing is happening. You may even feel empty when you're practicing stillness. But I promise you, if you will give yourself to this discipline and just do it—don't just try it, but build it into your lifestyle—over time you will experience a greater sense of God's peace and power, and you will come to know Him in a deeper way.

God says it for a reason: "Be still, and know that I am God."

> *Father God, I choose to be still before You, to cease my striving so I can experience Your movement in my life. I want to know You in a deeper way and be a vessel through which You can manifest Your power and goodness. Be magnified in my life.*

Nothing Is Wasted

And we know that all things work together for good to those who love God, to those who are the called according to His purpose.
—ROMANS 8:28, NKJV

YOU'RE PROBABLY FAMILIAR with Romans 8:28, where the Lord says He causes all things to work together for good to those who love Him and are called according to His purpose. Oftentimes we interpret that verse to mean that no matter what happens in life, God is going to use it for good. And that is absolutely true. But I want to draw your attention to the very next verse, Romans 8:29, because it reveals what God's purpose is—that we would be "conformed to the image of His Son" (NKJV).

Everything that you and I go through in life is going to be used by Father God to conform us to the image of His Son. What does that look like in our everyday lives? Let's say I am seventy-five years old, and because I'm old, I lose a tooth. Should I think, "This is going to work together for my good; I may even grow a brand-new tooth"?

Some people apply that verse that way. They think that no matter what happens, they're going to experience something better or somehow their circumstance will supernaturally improve. But that isn't exactly what Paul is saying. Paul is saying that God is going to use everything you go through in life for good by using everything to conform you to the image of Jesus and fulfill His purpose in your life.

Please keep in mind that God's ways are above our ways, even "as the heavens are higher than the earth" (Isa. 55:9, NKJV). And not only are His ways higher; His purpose for you and me is greater than the purpose we have for ourselves. His purpose is to conform us to the image of Jesus, which is why nothing we go through in life will ever be wasted.

> *Father God, I thank You that all things work together for my good and that You are using everything I go through to bring about Your purpose for my life, which is to conform me to the image of Your Son. Have Your way in my life today.*

God's Spirit Is in You

However, you are not in the flesh but in the Spirit, if indeed the Spirit of God dwells in you. But if anyone does not have the Spirit of Christ, he does not belong to Him.

—ROMANS 8:9

SOMETIMES WHEN WE hear certain words, they bring up preconceived notions that cause us to miss what is being communicated to us. *Born again* is that kind of term. The minute some people hear the phrase *born-again Christian*, they think of people who are extreme in their thinking, judgmental, or on the Far Right. But that is not what the term *born again* means. In fact from my perspective it is a scientific term.

Jesus said, "Unless one is born again he cannot see the kingdom of God" (John 3:3). He went on to say, "Truly, I say to you, unless one is born of water and the Spirit he cannot enter into the kingdom of God. That which is born of the flesh is flesh, and that which is born of the Spirit is spirit" (John 3:5–6). So when Jesus used the term *born again*, He wasn't just talking about a change of lifestyle or a new beginning. He was talking about literally being born of God's Spirit.

You see, there is a first birth and a second birth. The first birth is when you were born from your mother's womb. But when you receive Jesus, God's Spirit literally comes inside you. And when that happens, you receive another nature—God's own nature—because His Spirit comes and inhabits you. This is what the term *born again* actually means.

This is our reality as believers in Yeshua: those who belong to Christ—those who have been born again— have the Spirit of God living within them. We need to become less focused on what is going on outside of us and be more conscious of God's Spirit that dwells inside of us. This is how the early believers were able to do supernatural things—because they understood that God's Spirit literally lived inside them.

Let us not allow the world's concept of being born again keep us from understanding what Jesus truly meant. God's Spirit is in you. Begin to focus on that truth and ask the Father to bring that reality alive in your heart.

> *Father God, I believe and declare that Your Spirit is alive in me. Deepen my awareness of this reality, and move powerfully through me. Raise my expectation of what You can and will do in my life.*

DAY 5

The Greatest Victory

Beyond all these things put on love, which is the perfect bond of unity.

—Colossians 3:14

THROUGHOUT HIS LETTERS Paul tells us that love is above all else. Yet for many years as a young believer I didn't think much about love. I just thought about conquering. You know how men can be; we like to conquer, and as believers in Yeshua we are given power to conquer in life—to overcome trials, temptations, and the powers of darkness. But that is not our greatest strength. The greatest gift we have been given is the ability to love.

I want to encourage you today to think about this: if we are not walking in love, we are not abiding in Yeshua, because He is love. One of our missions as followers of Christ is to overcome evil with good, and the greatest good of all is love. In life there's so much division, so much criticism, so much accusation. But criticism and accusation are not from the Lord. They are from the enemy. Love brings people together.

If you can walk in love, you'll walk in victory. But walking in love is a choice. Love isn't a feeling; love is a choice. Jesus asked, What credit is it to us if we only love our friends? (See Luke 6:32–36.) It feels good to love our friends, but Jesus is calling us to overcome and conquer. He's calling us to love our enemies. He's calling us to choose to walk in love.

Often that means doing what we don't feel like doing. Jesus modeled that kind of love when He was about to go to the cross. He said, "Father, if it is possible, let this cup pass from Me; yet not as I will, but as You will" (Matt. 26:39). Jesus didn't want to die on the cross, but because of His love for the Father He did what He didn't feel like doing and gave His life for us.

In the same way, beloved, we need to choose love, even when it doesn't feel good. We need to overcome evil with good. We need to learn to overlook offense. We need to bring people together in unity. Unity brings life; division causes death. We need to walk in love. If you can do this, you'll have achieved the greatest victory of all.

> *Father God, thank You for humbling Yourself and dying on the cross for my sins. As You chose love, even when it hurt, I now choose to love those around me. I choose to cover them in prayer and bring people together in unity. I choose to walk in love.*

Keep Trusting God

> He saved us, not on the basis of deeds which we have done in righteousness, but according to His mercy, by the washing of regeneration and renewing by the Holy Spirit.
>
> —TITUS 3:5

SO MANY PEOPLE never feel secure in their walk with God. They think that somehow their salvation depends on their works, but Paul wrote in Titus 3 that God saved us not on the basis of our deeds but according to His mercy through the regenerating power of the Holy Spirit. Many times we think we realize this, but our actions tell a different story.

I have seen so many people start off right. They hear the gospel message and accept Jesus as their Savior. But once they start going to church, they are told they should do this and they shouldn't do that. Soon what was begun in the mercy of God as they yielded to the Lord, they now try to perfect by good works.

Galatians 3:3 says that what was begun in the Spirit, we should not try to perfect with the flesh. We need to keep trusting God, to keep clinging to Him and abiding in Jesus by depending on Him. In this way we're being transformed from glory to glory.

Please don't misunderstand what I'm saying. It's very important to know right from wrong and to choose what is right. But we need to be dependent on the Holy Spirit, step by step and day by day, and not try to accomplish good things for Him in our flesh.

So I want to encourage you today to trust in God. Trust in the One who saved you to complete what He began. Open your heart to Him, and share your deepest secrets with Him. Ask Him for help as often as you need to. He who began a good work in you will complete it because He did not save you on the basis of your righteous deeds but by His mercy and by the regenerating power of the Holy Spirit. Trust in the Lord, my friend, and you will be blessed because God continuously blesses everyone who looks to Him.

Father God, I know it is not by my works that I am saved or made righteous but according to Your mercy and the regenerating power of the Holy Spirit. I trust You to complete the work You began in me. Help me not to seek to please and serve You in my own strength. Help me to always look to You to provide all I need and to empower me to impact Your kingdom.

DAY 7

God Will Provide

I have heard the grumblings of the sons of Israel; speak to them, saying, "At twilight you shall eat meat, and in the morning you shall be filled with bread; and you shall know that I am the LORD your God."

—EXODUS 16:12

AFTER GOD DELIVERED the Israelites from slavery in Egypt, He led them to the Promised Land through the wilderness. Along the way, the people began to grumble about not having enough to eat, and God responded to their complaints by supernaturally meeting their needs.

You may know the story. God provided quail in the evening, and supernatural manna appeared on the ground each morning. This happened six days a week for forty years. God provided for the Israelites in this way the entire time they wandered in the wilderness. When they entered the Promised Land, the supernatural manna stopped. But while they were in the wilderness and had no other means of support, God fed them with heavenly manna and divinely supplied meat.

This happened thousands of years ago. But I want you to know that God will do the same for you. You may not receive manna and quail, but when you face wilderness experiences, God will meet your needs. Remember, Jesus said not to worry about what you will eat or what you will drink because your Father knows you need these things; if you just seek Him first, He will supply all your needs (Matt. 6:25–33).

The apostle Paul wrote that the Old Testament, the Tanakh, was "written for our instruction, upon whom the ends of the ages have come" (1 Cor. 10:11). One of the things we learn from the Old Testament is that God supernaturally provides for His people. God provided for the children of Israel when they were wandering in the wilderness, and He will provide for you. Beloved, you can trust Him.

> *Father God, thank You for being my provider. As I seek first Your kingdom and Your righteousness, I trust that everything I need will be added to me. Even during wilderness seasons when You seem far away, I know I can trust You. You said You will never leave me nor forsake me. Thank You, Father, for supplying all my needs according to Your riches in glory.*

DAY 8

Don't Be Led by Your Feelings

But I say, walk by the Spirit, and you will not carry out the desire of the flesh. For the flesh sets its desire against the Spirit, and the Spirit against the flesh; for these are in opposition to one another, so that you may not do the things that you please.

—GALATIANS 5:16–17

THE APOSTLE PAUL says if we set our minds on the Spirit, we won't carry out the desires of the flesh. Yet it is incredible how many Christians willingly give themselves over to the things of the flesh. I want to remind you today that you have a choice in what you reap in life. God never told us that we can control what we feel, but He did tell us that we can control what we choose.

Too many Christians are being led by what they feel, but God never said, "Whosoever feels…"; God said, "Whosoever will…" (Rev. 22:17, KJV). Living by the Spirit involves actively choosing to follow Christ, not moving by our feelings. So I want to encourage you to not live by your emotions, to not live by your lust. You can't expect to sow to the flesh and reap blessings from the Spirit of God. Galatians 6:8 says that "the one who sows to his own flesh will from the flesh reap corruption, but the one who sows to the Spirit will from the Spirit reap eternal life."

If you sow to the Spirit, you are going to reap love, joy, and peace, but sowing to the Spirit involves disciplining the will. Jesus paid a great price when He sacrificed Himself on the cross. He took nails in His hands, a spear in His side, and more nails in His feet. Living a godly life takes sacrifice too. It even hurts. Our flesh will want to avoid pain and discomfort at all costs, but we must discipline ourselves for the purpose of godliness.

You have a choice to make: whether to live by the flesh or by the Spirit. I encourage you to follow what is right, not what you feel. Feelings come and go, and they will deceive us. But the Spirit of God will lead us to experience blessing and eternal life. Don't grow weary in doing good. If you are faithful until the end, you shall reap a great reward!

Father God, help me to discipline myself to sow to the Spirit and not fulfill the lusts of the flesh. Help me choose to follow Your Spirit so that I may reap love, joy, peace, and eternal life.

Repentance Comes Before Blessing

For if you truly amend your ways and your deeds, if you truly practice justice between a man and his neighbor, if you do not oppress the alien, the orphan, or the widow, and do not shed innocent blood in this place, nor walk after other gods to your own ruin, then I will let you dwell in this place, in the land that I gave to your fathers forever and ever.

—JEREMIAH 7:5–7

IT IS IMPORTANT for us to understand that the Father's love for us is unconditional. But sometimes people today are so grace-oriented that they do not understand the power and necessity of repentance. They don't seem to realize it's the grace of God that leads us to repentance.

In order for us to experience God's presence consistently, we have to repent. This truth is seen throughout the New Testament. John the Baptist's message was "Repent, for the kingdom of heaven is at hand" (Matt.

3:2). And Jesus taught the same thing. (See Matthew 4:17.) But this concept is not only found in the New Testament. We see it also in the Hebrew Scriptures. Jeremiah said if the people of Israel would truly amend their ways (i.e., repent), and if they practiced justice; did not oppress the alien, the orphan, or the widow; and did not shed innocent blood or follow after false gods—all of which represent a turn toward God's way of doing things—then God would let them dwell in the land He gave their fathers forever and ever. The point is that repentance was required for people to receive the fullness of God's blessing.

Please hear me today: God loves us so much, but we need to put Him first in our lives and seek after Jesus. When we do this, the Spirit of the Lord is going to draw closer and closer to us, and we are going to experience His glory and His pleasure more and more. You see, we are partners with God. God does His part, but we have to do our part. Repentance precedes the blessing of God. "Draw near to God and He will draw near to you" (Jas. 4:8).

> *Father God, I receive Your Word. Help me to follow Your narrow way and to never despise Your chastening. Help me to be sensitive to Your conviction and quick to repent when I stray from Your will. I long to draw close to You and live in the fullness of Your blessing and power.*

The Deep Fellowship of His Love

Then you will call upon Me and come and pray to Me, and I will listen to you. You will seek Me and find Me when you search for Me with all your heart.

—JEREMIAH 29:12–13

THIS IS A beautiful passage of Scripture. It reminds us that when we seek God, we will find Him. Jesus said something similar in John 14:21–23:

"He who has My commandments and keeps them is the one who loves Me; and he who loves Me will be loved by My Father, and I will love him and will disclose Myself to him." Judas (not Iscariot) said to Him, "Lord, what then has happened that You are going to disclose Yourself to us and not to the world?" Jesus answered and said to him, "If anyone loves Me, he will keep My word; and My Father will love him, and We will come to him and make Our abode with him."

Jesus was saying in essence, if you love Me, keep My Word, and obey Me, you'll be loved by My Father, and you'll experience Our presence and Our love for you.

These verses in Jeremiah and in John are not saying God's love is determined by your obedience. God's love is unconditional. But when you love Him by obeying Him, He responds to you by giving you the opportunity to experience deep fellowship with Him in a consciousness of His love and supernatural presence. In other words, you will know Him in a deeper way because He will reveal Himself to you so you can feel His love.

So many people think God is angry with them, but He loves us more than we can comprehend. Beloved, if you long to experience the deep fellowship of the Father's love, seek Him with all your heart. If you do, you will find Him.

Father God, I need to feel Your love. I need to experience Your presence. More than anything else in life, I need You, Father God. So, Father, if there's anything in my life that's preventing me from entering into deeper fellowship with You, if there's anything that's in the way, put Your finger on it now by the power of the Holy Spirit. Break it up by Your power, O God, and release me to run deep into Your arms so I can know You fully, completely, and truly.

Seize God's Word

The grass withers, the flower fades, but the word
of our God stands forever.

—ISAIAH 40:8

MANY YEARS AGO the Lord spoke to me audibly. This doesn't happen to me all the time, but it has happened a few times in my life, including on this particular occasion. I clearly heard the Lord say, "Seize My Word and don't let anything else in."

The word felt like a river of fire rolling through my soul. It was so powerful, yet I struggled with what God said. I asked Him, "What are You saying to me, Lord? How do I seize Your Word?" I thought, "This is Your Word right here, the Bible, and it is a big book. How do I seize the whole thing?" I couldn't quite wrap my head around what God was saying.

But after some time this is what I came to realize. The grass withers, and the flowers fade—temporary circumstances of life come and go—but the Word in us will abide, and it will enable us to stand and be victorious in life. When we seize the Word, we won't allow ourselves to be moved by temporary things. Life is always changing. The situations in which we find ourselves are always going to change. So if we allow ourselves to become victims of our circumstances, we will end up on an emotional roller coaster and always weak in faith. But when we seize God's Word and refuse to let anything else in, we will become strong, solid believers.

Jesus said, "The words that I speak to you are spirit, and they are life" (John 6:63, NKJV). So if you are facing something in the natural that is making you anxious and fearful, remember that God's Word said for you to fear not because He is with you (Isa. 41:10). Remind yourself to be of good cheer, for He has overcome the world (John 16:33). In other words, choose to believe His Word. Don't allow what you see with your natural eyes to control your heart. Everything you see is temporary and will fade away. Beloved, make up your mind today to live not by what you see or feel but by the Word of God. I want to encourage you to begin each day by reading and seizing His Word.

> *Father God, I choose to put my confidence in You. I will not be moved by the temporary circumstances of life. I trust Your Word, for it is spirit, it is life, and it stands forever.*

Divine Satisfaction

All things are wearisome; man is not able to tell it. The eye is not satisfied with seeing, nor is the ear filled with hearing.

—ECCLESIASTES 1:8

THE THINGS OF the world can never fully satisfy. Now, I know that when we were young and we experienced things for the first time in life, that did feel satisfying, didn't it? I remember as a young person experiencing so many things for the first time and thinking life was such an adventure. The thing is, as we get older, those things are no longer new, and when the newness wears off, we find that the eye is not satisfied because it has already seen so much. The ear is not satisfied because it has already heard so much. The only place we find satisfaction that will increase and endure is in God.

Finding satisfaction is what the whole Book of Ecclesiastes is about. The story of Ecclesiastes is that the king went on a journey to satisfy himself, and he went after everything the world had to offer. He went after

wealth, after fame, after wisdom, after sexual relationships, hoping those things would satisfy him. But after
all of his pursuits he found that none of them filled him
up. He realized he was still empty.

I hope you have come to a place in your life where
you realize that there really is nothing worth living for
other than God Himself. Seek ye first the kingdom of
God, beloved ones, and God will bring divine satisfaction and stability into your life. I challenge you today to
ask yourself what you need to do to put the pursuit of
God first in your life. Remember, God is a rewarder of
those who diligently seek Him (Heb. 11:6). He is waiting
for you to seek satisfaction in Him, "the fountain of
living waters" (Jer. 2:13). Jesus said, "But whoever drinks
of the water that I will give him shall never thirst; but
the water that I will give him will become in him a well
of water springing up to eternal life" (John 4:14).

*Father God, I commit to putting my pur-
suit of You above all other pursuits because
nothing and no one else can truly satisfy. As
Psalm 107:9 declares, You fill the hungry soul
with good things. I choose to be satisfied with
You.*

Suffering for Righteousness' Sake

But even if you should suffer for the sake of righteousness, you are blessed. And do not fear their intimidation, and do not be troubled.

—1 PETER 3:14

THERE WILL BE times when you will be rejected because of your faith in Jesus. Persecution will come. But I want you to understand that there is nothing to fear when these things happen. When you suffer because of your love for God and your faithfulness to His Word, you will experience a closeness and a deep fellowship with God that can't be experienced when life is easy. Peter told us that even if we suffer, if we're doing it for righteousness' sake, we are blessed.

You see, Jesus said, "Blessed are those who are persecuted for righteousness' sake" (Matt. 5:10, NKJV). We often feel closest to God when we are going through trials. I believe this is because God condescends to meet us when we are weak. This is why Paul said he would rather boast in his weakness. He said, "[God] has said to me, 'My grace is sufficient for you, for power is perfected in weakness.' Most gladly, therefore, I will rather boast about my weaknesses, so that the power of Christ may dwell in me. Therefore I am well content with weaknesses, with insults, with distresses, with persecutions, with difficulties, for Christ's sake; *for when I am weak, then I am strong*" (2 Cor. 12:9–10, emphasis added). The Christian life will never be easy, but God's power is perfected in our weakness.

Don't be afraid of the world. Don't be intimidated by the agnostics, the atheists, and those who call Christians narrow-minded haters because we proclaim that Jesus is the only way. Do not back down. You're going to be rejected. You're going to be persecuted. Jesus said, "'A servant is not greater than his master.' If they persecuted Me, they will also persecute you" (John 15:20, NKJV). Beloved, you have been chosen by God not just to reign with Jesus but to suffer with Him as well. But don't be afraid. Be a soldier. Be willing to take some blows because of your love for Jesus and your defense of the gospel. You are going to be rewarded for it. Be strong and courageous in your love of God.

> *Father God, I know that Yeshua suffered for the sake of the gospel, and I will suffer at times as well. Help me to be courageous and never back down from proclaiming Your Word.*

God Chose You

> But you are a chosen race, a royal priesthood, a holy nation, a people for God's own possession, so that you may proclaim the excellencies of Him who has called you out of darkness into His marvelous light.
>
> —1 Peter 2:9

GOD CHOSE YOU. Pause for a minute and let that sink in. You have been chosen by the all-knowing, all-powerful God. You are special. The Lord actually says that we're a chosen race, a royal priesthood, a holy nation. To be holy means you are unique. You are cut out. You are set apart. Please don't just gloss over those statements, because truly believing those truths can transform your life.

Knowing that God chose you is the antidote to low self-esteem and the cure for feelings of inferiority and insignificance. It is how you become a bold witness for the Lord. Jesus said in John 15:16, "You did not choose Me but I *chose you*" (emphasis added). When you truly believe you are chosen by God, beloved one, it's going to activate something in you. It's going to give you supernatural courage and confidence. When you know that like Jeremiah you were chosen from your mother's womb, when you truly know that, it's going to supernaturally cause you to become a radical follower of Jesus.

When you realize that He loves you so much that He chose you for a very special relationship with Him, it will awaken in your heart a deep love for Him. And it will cause you to realize you have a destiny because God didn't just choose you; He chose you for a purpose. He chose you "that you may proclaim the excellencies of Him who has called you out of darkness into His marvelous light."

You are special to God. He chose you to be a light in this world. Begin to walk in that truth.

Father God, thank You for choosing me and for setting me apart for Your purpose. I choose to believe I am special to You, and I will proclaim the excellencies of Messiah Jesus, who brought me out of darkness and into Your marvelous light. Help me to be a light in the earth today. Empower me by Your Spirit to be a witness for You.

Touch the Father With Your Praise

Let everything that has breath praise the LORD.
Praise the LORD!

—PSALM 150:6

ONE DAY SOON you and I are going to be in an environment where the words of Psalm 150:6 will be a reality. In heaven everything that has breath will be praising the Lord. We won't be able to help it. Praise will be involuntary just as breathing is involuntary. Praise will simply be the natural response to the greatness and glory of God.

But on earth right now we have a choice. We can either choose to grumble, focus on the negative, and see the glass as only half full, or we can count our blessings and wake up in the morning, saying: "Father God, I thank You that I am alive today and that You have given me an opportunity to grow in You. I thank You, Father God, that even though things are difficult, You are using these challenges to strengthen me, and this season is producing an eternal weight of glory in me that cannot compare to the temporary difficulty."

Beloved, God has given you the power to touch His heart through your praise. So I want to encourage you to choose to praise God while you are on this earth. Show the Father that you love Him by being positive and blessing Him. Yeshua loves you so much, and when you pour out your love for Him through your praise, it moves His heart.

Father God, You are great and greatly to be praised. I know that one day everything that has breath will be praising You in heaven, but I choose to praise You now. You have been too good for me to keep silent. You have given me life and strength, and You sacrificed Your Son so I could spend eternity with You. Father, You are worthy of my praise. Help me to never take Your goodness to me for granted.

DAY 16

Love = Obedience

Not everyone who says to Me, "Lord, Lord," will enter the kingdom of heaven, but he who does the will of My Father who is in heaven will enter.

—MATTHEW 7:21

I THINK SOMETIMES WE get confused about what it really means to love God. Sometimes we feel we love God because we're singing a worship song, our hands are raised, and we're feeling blessed by the beautiful worship music. Our hearts may be moved, and tears may come to our eyes, but I want you to know that loving God is not foremost about experiencing His Spirit's presence through worship. People who really love God obey Him.

Jesus said in John 14:21, "He who has My commandments and keeps them is the one who loves Me." He didn't say, "He who loves me will shed tears during the worship service." Believe me, I know and agree that it is awesome to be touched by God while singing a worship song, but loving God is not first about feeling something. Love is primarily a decision of the will, and it is demonstrated through obedience.

This is seen throughout the Scriptures. The children of Israel were commanded to "love the Lord your God, and always keep His charge, His statutes, His ordinances, and His commandments" (Deut. 11:1). And John wrote that "this is love, that we walk according to His commandments" (2 John 6). Again and again, loving God is linked to obedience.

Beloved, don't be dependent on feelings. Make being obedient the primary focus of your life.

Father God, help me to love You with my obedience. Make me sensitive to Your Spirit so I can follow Your leading and not go my own way. Impart to me a holy fear of You, and train me to walk by faith and truth rather than by my feelings. Father, help me to love You with my life.

An Anchor for the Soul

This hope we have as an anchor of the soul, a hope both sure and steadfast and one which enters within the veil, where Jesus has entered as a forerunner for us, having become a high priest forever according to the order of Melchizedek.

—HEBREWS 6:19–20

NO MATTER WHERE you find yourself in your journey today, tomorrow, or even next year, you can enter into God's holy presence because Jesus made a way for you by dying for your sins and then being raised up into the presence of God the Father for your justification.

Because Yeshua shed His blood on the cross, your ability to enter into the presence of God is sure and strong. You can go into God's presence, draw near to Him, and cry out to Him for help. Accessing the presence of God does not depend on your deeds. If it did, your access would not be sure and strong, because you don't know what you are going to do tomorrow. You may lose your temper. You may scream at someone or do something selfish. But because your ability to go before the Father is not dependent on the deeds of righteousness you have done but is according to His mercy and what Jesus has done, as Titus 3:5 says, you can go before Him anytime, and He will be there. This promise is sure and strong, and it is never going to change.

God loves you just as much right now as He will love you tomorrow and the next day and next month and next year. He will never love you any more or less than He does right now, and your ability to be near Him will always be because of Jesus. Beloved, Jesus is your lifeline. Cling to Him with all your strength, for if you set your hope on Him, you will not be disappointed. (See Isaiah 49:23, NIV.)

> *Father God, thank You for loving me and for making it possible for me to be in Your presence. I thank You that my access to You is not dependent on my behavior but only on what You have done for me on the cross. Thank You for being an anchor for my soul, a hope both sure and steadfast.*

DAY 18

Don't Live for Yourself

Know therefore that the LORD your God, He is God, the faithful God, who keeps His covenant and His lovingkindness to a thousandth generation with those who love Him and keep His commandments.

—DEUTERONOMY 7:9

BELOVED, YOUR WALK with God affects more than just you. This is what the Torah is telling us in Deuteronomy 7:9. When we who have influence over other people's lives are walking with God, the blessing on our lives spills down into the lives of those around us.

In this particular scripture the Lord is speaking about generational blessing. But I believe that in a more general way God uses each of us to bring sanctification, if not entirely then partially, to those who are close to us. This is evident in the New Testament when the apostle Paul says a believer who is married to an unbeliever can be a source of sanctification for the unbelieving spouse (1 Cor. 7:13–14).

Your relationship with God has a much bigger impact

than you probably think. You are not serving God just so you can live a blessed life in Him. Your relationship with God is also blessing those around you. You can be a source of light to many. So don't just live for yourself. Don't just think about your needs or wants. Think bigger. Be mindful of the impact your choices today will have on those around you and even future generations.

Soon we are going to be standing before Jesus being rewarded according to what we have done. So I encourage you today to live for God. Be a light. Sometimes it will bring people to Yeshua, sometimes it will separate you from close relationships, but it will always matter for eternity. God is going to use you to touch lives.

Father God, help me to realize the power that I have in and through You to affect and bless others.

God Loves You More Than You Know

And because you are sons, God has sent forth the Spirit of His Son into your hearts, crying out, "Abba, Father!"

—GALATIANS 4:6, NKJV

THE BIBLE SAYS we have received the spirit of adoption by which we cry out, "Abba, Father" (Rom. 8:15). It is important for us to recognize that God is not just some Being in the sky somewhere whom we can pray to when we have a need. No, He saved you and me to bring us into a son/daughter relationship with Him.

When the Father brought us to Himself, He placed us in Jesus. And because you and I are in Jesus, we are God's sons and daughters. Can you comprehend the magnitude of that?

Think about this: All the Father's love is focused on Jesus—He is the Son of God. Jesus is in the bosom of the Father, and it has always been that way. All the Father's love is focused on Him, but you are now in

Jesus, and because of that all His love is focused on you in like manner.

I want you to know today, beloved, that the Father loves you and me with a love that is hard to comprehend. But we should pray to understand it—"that you, being rooted and grounded in love, may be able to comprehend with all the saints what is the breadth and length and height and depth, and to know the love of Christ which surpasses knowledge, that you may be filled up to all the fullness of God" (Eph. 3:17–19).

> *Father God, I long to know the breadth and length and height and depth of Your love, though it surpasses my ability to comprehend. I ask that You deepen my understanding of Your heart for me. I pray that You will fill me up with the fullness of who You are.*

Tell Him You Need Him

> But when Jesus heard this, He said, "It is not those who are healthy who need a physician, but those who are sick. But go and learn what this means: 'I desire compassion, and not sacrifice,' for I did not come to call the righteous, but sinners."
>
> —Matthew 9:12–13

It may seem obvious, but today's passage reveals an important truth: Jesus just wants us to recognize that we need Him. He did not come for the righteous but for sinners; He came for those who know they are sick. This tells us, beloved, that we do not have to be perfect to go before God. He already knows we're not perfect.

Jesus loves and accepts you just as you are. His death on the cross built a bridge that enables you to receive the fullness of the Father's love right where you are. God is never going to love you any more or less than He loves you right now. But please hear me when I say this: He loves you and me too much to leave us where we are. He wants to conform us to the image of His dear Son, as Romans 8:29 says.

God doesn't expect us to be perfect, but He does expect us to be transparent before Him. He wants us to be open with Him so He can work in the areas of our lives that need healing and deliverance. That is my challenge to you today. Be open and vulnerable before God. Tell Him how much you need Him. Tell Him what is wrong in your life. Tell Him where you need help, because Jesus said He did not come for those who are well but for those who need a physician.

Talk to God every day and tell Him where it hurts. Tell Him where you are sick. Tell Him where you need help. If you are struggling with an area of sin, be open and honest. Cry out to God. When you do, God will transform your life, because He came for those who know they are sick and choose to turn to Him.

> *Father, forgive me for not always being honest with You about myself. I need You. I love You. Help me in Messiah Jesus' name.*

Trials Are a Gift

> Consider it all joy, my brethren, when you encounter various trials, knowing that the testing of your faith produces endurance. And let endurance have its perfect result, so that you may be perfect and complete, lacking in nothing.
>
> —JAMES 1:2–4

JAMES SAID TO consider it joy when you are facing trials, because the testing of your faith produces endurance and makes you complete in Him.

You see, beloved, trials are God's gift to us to make us strong. It's just like when people are getting in shape physically. In order to build their physical muscles, they have to face resistance. That's why weight training is also called resistance training. Pushing past our comfort zones increases our capacity.

So whether in the natural or in the spirit, the way to grow stronger is to face resistance. That is why James says to consider it joy when we face trials. Those trials serve to bring us into a deeper peace in Jesus. They make us complete.

Every day, all day long, life is a trial. That's the truth. Sure, we have seasons when we are just lying in the sun being blessed and refreshed, but generally speaking, life is a trial. We have to choose the right thoughts to think all day long, and the enemy is always trying to make us worry, make us fear, and give us wrong perceptions of reality. All day long we have to battle to stay in peace and to choose God. We have to pray for wisdom and understanding so we can overcome in the love of God and be brought into His victory.

I want to encourage you with this: Life is meant to be a battle; it is meant to be a trial. We need adversity to become strong, and as we get strong, we are made happy.

Father God, I will try to receive trials as a gift from You and trust that You have a purpose for them.

The Path That Leads to Life

> The fear of the LORD is the beginning of
> wisdom, and the knowledge of the Holy One is
> understanding.
>
> —PROVERBS 9:10

WE LIVE IN a Christian culture that has begun to stress grace to such a degree that we are afraid to talk about the fear of the Lord. But I want you to know, beloved, that the grace of God is not opposed to the fear of the Lord. In fact to fear the Lord is actually a gift of God's grace because the fear of the Lord is the beginning of wisdom. This is why the psalmist said, "Let all the earth fear the LORD.... Behold, the eye of the LORD is on those who fear Him" (Ps. 33:8, 18).

In the Book of Romans, which is the most precise theological treatise in the entire New Testament, the apostle Paul shows humankind that we are guilty before God and in danger of eternal death. It is only after Paul points out that we have all sinned and fallen short of the glory of God that he presents the solution: Yeshua (Rom. 3:23–24). But today we don't want to talk about people being guilty in their sin. We don't want to talk about hell, and we often don't want to talk about the fear of the Lord. We just want to talk about how much God loves everyone and all the good things He wants to do for us.

It is 100 percent true that God loves us and desires to give good gifts to His children. But we need to be biblical in our approach. Jesus said that unless we repent, we will perish (Luke 13:5). Perhaps this is why Psalm 19:9 says, "The fear of the LORD is clean, enduring forever."

So today I want to remind you that the fear of the Lord is a beautiful thing. God does not want us to be afraid of Him. But a healthy fear of the Lord is God's gift to you because, as Proverbs 19:23 says, it keeps you walking down the straight path that leads to life, and "the secret of the LORD is for those who fear Him" (Ps. 25:14).

> *Father God, You are worthy of all honor. Awaken in my heart a healthy fear of You. Your Word says, "How blessed is everyone who fears the LORD" (Ps. 128:1). Help me to fully embrace this gift that will keep me on the path that leads to life.*

God Is With You

Where can I go from Your Spirit? Or where can I flee from Your presence? If I ascend to heaven, You are there; if I make my bed in Sheol, behold, You are there.

—PSALM 139:7–8

WE LOVE THE entire Bible, but many of us, if we're honest, have favorite parts. Psalm 139:7–8 is one of my favorite passages of Scripture because it lets us know that wherever we are, God is there. There is no place we can go in life where God is absent, so we never have to be afraid that we can be somewhere God is not. God will always be with us, no matter what happens to us in life.

Home is where God is, and because God is always with us, we can always be at home. If you're afraid of something, remember that God is with you. Most of the things we fear pertain to the future. The problem is when we have anxious thoughts about the future, the element that is often left out of the equation is God. We do not consider that He will be with us in the situation. Let me give you an example to help you understand.

I heard about a woman who was fearful every single day that she was going to lose her job. For months she was afraid that her boss was going to fire her. I mean it kept her up at night. Then one day her boss called the woman into the office and fired her. But when she got fired, she had total peace. Why? Because when she got fired, God's presence was with her.

You see, when we fear the future, God is usually absent from our thoughts. But God is going to be with you in your future, and when you are in the future with God's presence surrounding you, you won't be afraid. Jesus said, "I am with you always, even to the end of the age" (Matt. 28:20). He will never leave us nor forsake us (Deut. 31:6; Heb. 13:5).

There is no place you can go to get away from God. He is always with you.

> *Father, I thank You for being with me wher-*
> *ever I go. I cannot hide from Your Spirit, nor*
> *can I flee from Your presence. I thank You*
> *that You will never leave me nor forsake me.*
> *When I feel afraid, help me to remember that*
> *You are with me and always will be.*

DAY 24

The Greatest Gift

God has raised this Jesus to life, and we are all witnesses of it. Exalted to the right hand of God, he has received from the Father the promised Holy Spirit and has poured out what you now see and hear.

—ACTS 2:32–33, NIV

IN ACTS 2 Peter is preaching to the crowd that gathered after the power of the Holy Spirit was poured out on the disciples in the Upper Room. When those first believers received the Holy Spirit, their lives supernaturally changed, and the same thing happens to you and me, beloved.

When you are empowered by the Holy Spirit, there will be a supernatural dimension to your life. The Spirit of the living God, the Ruach HaKodesh, makes us alive. He gives us revelation into the heart of God so we can know Him. The Spirit of God will also give us supernatural boldness, supernatural peace, supernatural joy, and supernatural revelation. God's Spirit imparts to us a supernatural ability to love, overcome, and prosper.

In Hebrew we call the Holy Spirit the Ruach HaKodesh, which means the breath of God. There is no greater gift God could give than His own Spirit.

Thank You, Father God, for giving me Your Spirit, for empowering me with the Ruach HaKodesh, and making me a bold witness for You. I ask that You allow me to experience the supernatural. Use me to manifest Your glory in the earth.

Guard Your Heart From Fear

For God has not given us a spirit of fear, but of
power and of love and of a sound mind.
—2 Timothy 1:7, nkjv

THE BIBLE MAKES it clear that we wrestle not against
flesh and blood. We are battling "spiritual forces of
wickedness" (Eph. 6:12). Demonic spirits gain access to
our lives in a variety of ways. You may already know
that you can open doors to these spirits when you
come into agreement with sin and lies, and that sometimes demonic spirits run in families. But many people
don't realize that demons also gain access to our lives
through fear.

Even as faith opens a channel for the Spirit of God
to operate through you, fear opens up a channel for the
powers of darkness to gain access to your life. The Bible
tells us more than one hundred times to fear not. The
Lord said not to call a conspiracy what the world calls
a conspiracy, and "you are not to fear what they fear
or be in dread of it." Instead, "it is the Lord of hosts

whom you should regard as holy. And He shall be your fear, and He shall be your dread" (Isa. 8:12–13).

When you fear God alone, He will become a sanctuary for you. In Him you will find peace and strength. And you can declare with David the promise in Psalm 27, "In the day of trouble He will conceal me in His tabernacle; in the secret place of His tent He will hide me; He will lift me up on a rock. And now my head will be lifted up above my enemies around me, and I will offer in His tent sacrifices with shouts of joy; I will sing, yes, I will sing praises to the LORD" (vv. 5–6).

Remember the words of the Father: "Do not fear, for I am with you; do not anxiously look about you, for I am your God. I will strengthen you, surely I will help you, surely I will uphold you with My righteous right hand" (Isa. 41:10). I want to encourage you to break fear off your life. Begin to take authority over it in the name of Jesus. And guard your heart against the spirit of fear. The more your words and thoughts fall out of sync with fear, the freer and freer you will become.

> *Father, in Messiah Jesus' name I ask You to strengthen me. Teach me how to guard my heart from fear. I take authority over fear in the mighty name of Yeshua.*

DAY 26

Choose to Overcome

No temptation has overtaken you but such as is common to man; and God is faithful, who will not allow you to be tempted beyond what you are able, but with the temptation will provide the way of escape also, so that you will be able to endure it.

—1 Corinthians 10:13

LIFE IS A test. What do I mean by that? God has given us a free will, and every experience we have in life is an opportunity to choose how we are going to respond. The Lord wants us to cling to Him continually, to look to Him for wisdom and strength to handle every temptation and trial, so that we overcome.

In 1 Corinthians 10:13 the Lord is telling us that trials and temptations are common to man and that we don't have to face them without Him. Nothing you will face in life is so unique that no one has ever dealt with it before. All trials have varieties of color, but at the end of the day they are similar at the root. The difference is in how we choose to handle them.

God wants you to choose to overcome—to not lose yourself in frustration but to respond in peace. He wants you to choose to overcome in love, in faith, and with a sound mind. Every time you choose correctly, you get stronger in the spirit and ascend further into the light.

I want to encourage you to realize that all the challenges, all the temptations, all the trials in life are tests. Be cognizant of that at all times because Revelation 2:7 tells us that he who overcomes will inherit the paradise of God. We need to choose God all day and every day because to the degree that we do, we will be rewarded and shine in His glory forever and ever.

Father, I thank You that You have made a way for me to be victorious in life. Help me to choose to overcome—to choose Your ways and not my own, to follow Your Spirit and not my flesh. Help me to endure hardship as a good soldier.

DAY 27

Move With the Cloud

Throughout all their journeys whenever the cloud was taken up from over the tabernacle, the sons of Israel would set out; but if the cloud was not taken up, then they did not set out until the day when it was taken up.

—Exodus 40:36–37

WHILE THE ISRAELITES were wandering in the wilderness, they carried a tabernacle with them. God gave them specific instructions for how the tabernacle should be designed in order for God's presence to rest over this portable sanctuary as a cloud during the day and a pillar of fire at night. Whenever the cloud or the pillar of fire stopped, they would set up camp and remain in that location as long as the fire and the cloud stayed in that place. But as soon as it moved, the children of Israel immediately packed up camp and followed the cloud or the pillar of fire wherever it went.

In doing this, the Lord was training His people to be sensitive to His Spirit. They never knew when the cloud or the fire was going to lift, and they never knew where it was going to set. They could be traveling again in two days, two months, or two years—they never knew what was coming next. They had to be ready 24/7 to instantly obey the Lord.

Beloved, that is how the Lord wants us to be. He wants us to be flexible and obey His voice immediately and be led by His Spirit. God does not follow our human logic. He makes the last first and the first last, and He says the least will be the greatest. He chooses the foolish things of the world to confound the wise. We cannot put God in a box, nor can we figure Him out, so let's stop trying.

The children of Israel never knew when the fire or the cloud would lift or where it would go, and they had to obey God at a moment's notice—and that is how God wants us to be. He wants us to move with the cloud because as we obey God, miracles will happen in our lives.

> *Father God, help me to be sensitive to Your Spirit. As the Israelites moved with the cloud by day and the fire by night when they were wandering in the wilderness, help me to respond to Your leading as soon as You speak. I ask, Father, that You sharpen my discernment so I will be better able to recognize Your voice.*

He Alone Is God

Hear, O Israel! The LORD is our God, the LORD is one!

—DEUTERONOMY 6:4

IN JUDAISM THE most famous declaration from the Torah is found in Deuteronomy 6:4, and it is called the Shema: "Hear, O Israel! The LORD is our God, the LORD is one!" The Hebrew word translated "one" in that verse is *echad*. Often Jewish people say they can't believe in Jesus because there's only one God, and Christians speak of three Gods: the Father, the Son, and the Holy Spirit. But, beloved, let me make myself clear: Christians are not talking about three Gods. We worship only one God who is multidimensional.

You see, the Bible says that from the very beginning the Son has been in the bosom of the Father (John 1:18). And when we study the Hebrew word *echad* in the Torah, we find that it is often used to denote multidimensional unity as opposed to a singular unity. For example, in Genesis 2:24, where we read that "a man shall leave his father and his mother, and be joined to his wife; and they shall become one flesh," the Hebrew word translated "one" is *echad*. So what we have is a man and woman, two different people, being joined together as one.

Deuteronomy 6:4 is not proclaiming that God is a singular unity. Rather, I believe the Lord is saying that He alone is God! In fact in some Bible versions the Shema is translated as "The LORD is our God, the LORD alone" (e.g., NLT).

Beloved, there is only one God, as 1 Timothy 2:5 says: "For there is one God, and one mediator also between God and men, the man Christ Jesus." God is multidimensional, but He is one, and He alone is God.

> *Father, I thank You for the multidimensional unity exhibited in the Godhead. You exist eternally as the Father, Son, and Holy Spirit. I don't know how the Trinity works, but I know You alone are God, and I can count on You to be my Father, my Savior, and my Teacher. I love You, Lord, for being all that I need. In Jesus' name, amen.*

The Key to Divine Happiness

> How blessed is the man who does not walk in the counsel of the wicked, nor stand in the path of sinners, nor sit in the seat of scoffers! But his delight is in the law of the LORD, and in His law he meditates day and night.
>
> —PSALM 1:1–2

TODAY'S CULTURE IS, for the most part, hostile to the things of God. The Western world is increasingly opposed to Christian principles. But the Bible assures that when you refuse to follow the crowd, when you don't laugh at their jokes, when you don't listen to their music, when you don't adopt their sexual morals, but instead meditate on the Lord's law day and night, you will be blessed.

Now, what does the word *blessed* mean? To be blessed is to be divinely happy. Jesus said that unless we pick up our cross, deny ourselves, and follow Him, we can't be His disciples (Matt. 16:24). He also said that we need to follow His example and resist sin, even "to the point of shedding blood" (Heb. 12:4). This means that resisting sin is not going to be easy. But I want you to know, beloved, that if you will pick up your cross and follow the straight and narrow path that leads to life, it will be worth it. You are going to get to the end of your life and be so happy you chose to follow Him. You won't regret what you had to sacrifice.

Choosing to follow Jesus is the true key to happiness. Know that I love you and am cheering you on today to continue in your walk of faith.

Father God, Your Word says those who do not walk in the counsel of the ungodly will be blessed. So, Lord, I choose to focus on You and Your Word, and to delight in Your truth. Help me to be diligent in my walk of faith so I can experience the divine happiness promised in Your Word.

The Battle Is Not With Flesh and Blood

For our struggle is not against flesh and blood, but against the rulers, against the powers, against the world forces of this darkness, against the spiritual forces of wickedness in the heavenly places.
—EPHESIANS 6:12

THE BIBLE CLEARLY says we are in a fight that is invisible. But how many of us are still fighting against people and the things that we see? We're always mad at somebody—at our employer, at a colleague, at someone on our social media feed. But those people and situations are not the real problem. The real problem is how we are viewing our circumstances and how we are thinking about the obstacles we face.

Beloved, 99 percent of our battles are not flesh-and-blood struggles; they are battles in the realm of the mind. You see, thoughts are manifestations of spiritual activity, which is why we need to engage in spiritual warfare in the realm of our thought life.

Too many of us are allowing anything to captivate our thinking. We allow ourselves to dwell on whatever goes through our minds, not realizing that some of the thoughts we think and agree with actually have a satanic origin. You need to become aware of what you are thinking and understand that you have the power to reject and break agreement with thoughts that are not of God. That may mean speaking to your thoughts audibly and saying, "I reject you, Satan. Get out of my head!"

For so many years I accepted whatever thought came into my head, not realizing I had the power to fight it. I would cry out to God for help, but I didn't realize that I had the power to reject the thought and to focus on something different.

God has given you the tools to fight. Practice being aware of your thoughts, and forcefully reject anything that is not of the Lord. As you do, you will find yourself entering into greater and greater levels of shalom.

> *Father God, I ask that You give me a supernatural awareness of my thoughts. Help me to think on "whatever is true, whatever is honorable, whatever is right, whatever is pure, whatever is lovely, whatever is of good repute," as Philippians 4:8 admonishes. Father, help me to take captive any thought that is not in line with Your truth so I can experience peace and joy.*

DAY 31

Bear One Another's Burdens

Bear one another's burdens, and thereby fulfill
the law of Christ.

—Galatians 6:2

JESUS HAS MADE us members of His own body, and
He feels our pain. When we rejoice, He is happy. And
when we are hurting, He feels our sadness. He feels
what we feel and bears the weight of our joy or pain
with us.

This is what we are being called to do for one another
in Galatians 6:2. The Bible says we are members of one
another (Rom. 12:5), which means we are not meant to
live in our own little worlds. We are called to be conscious of other people's burdens and pain.

We live in a world that is so individualistic. People
are so separated from one another that many believers
don't do much in the way of bearing others' burdens.
Yes, we do need to be careful not to become over-
whelmed by people's problems. But most people have
the opposite problem. We don't let other people's problems touch us.

Beloved, God wants to help us to feel compassion for others, to try to put ourselves in their shoes. He wants to give us a greater burden to love, a greater burden to pray. He wants to bring us into a place where we can have more empathy for other people and thereby bear their burdens with them even as He is bearing our burdens with us.

We need discernment and balance, but we must not close ourselves off from being there for others. Let's do a better job of bearing one another's burdens by praying for one another and helping one another find strength through the power of the Spirit.

Father God, thank You for always being there to bear my burdens. Give me a heart to do the same for others. I pray for discernment and balance, Father, but help me not to shield myself from people's problems but to reach out to help them find strength in You.

Be Confident in Him

Therefore let us draw near with confidence to the throne of grace, so that we may receive mercy and find grace to help in time of need.

—HEBREWS 4:16

BECAUSE YESHUA HAS shed His blood for us, you and I can come boldly before the Father, free from condemnation. Through the blood of Jesus we stand before the Father, holy and blameless.

Jesus' blood has once and for all taken away the sin barrier between you and the Father. The stain of your past sins and your future sins has been removed by one act. By Jesus dying on the cross in your place, taking your sin into Himself, into His own body on the tree, you now have full access to the Father, and you stand holy and blameless before Him in love.

Because of Yeshua, when the Father looks at you, there is nothing in the way of His loving and accepting you. This is the difference between the Christian faith and every other faith in the world. Many other world religions promote beneficial truths, but they cannot lead you into the bosom of the Father, nor can they remove your sins. Only Yeshua the Messiah can do that.

I want you to know that the Father loves you. He loved you before you were born. That's why He sent Jesus to die for you. He wants you to come to Him, to run to Him today, and to have confidence in His love for you.

> *Father, thank You for Your great love for me. Thank You for sending Jesus to die for my sins so I can come before You, free of condemnation. Help me to have even more confidence in Your love.*

Let Peace Rule

Let the peace of Christ rule in your hearts...and
be thankful.

—Colossians 3:15

B ELOVED, GOD'S CALL upon your life and mine is
that we would have peace in Him. We're not going
to have peace in the world, but we can have peace in
Him.

But how do we experience that peace? One dimension of the answer is found in a familiar passage: "You
will keep him in perfect peace, whose mind is stayed
on You, because he trusts in You" (Isa. 26:3, NKJV).
The New American Standard Bible puts it this way:
"The steadfast of mind You will keep in perfect peace,
because he trusts in You." God promises that if we keep
our minds fixed, or steadfast, on Him, He will keep us
in perfect peace.

I know this is easier said than done. But I've found
that when I don't purposely focus on something, all
kinds of thoughts intrude on my mind. To remain in
peace, we must intentionally "set [our] mind on the

things above, not on the things that are on earth" (Col. 3:2). We must "[destroy] speculations and every lofty thing raised up against the knowledge of God, and… [take] every thought captive to the obedience of Christ" (2 Cor. 10:5).

Beloved, I want to encourage you to believe the peace of God instead of anxiety can rule your heart. No matter how long you've been battling, keep fighting the fight of faith. Be mindful of what you're thinking, and realize that if you're anxious, the spirit making you anxious is not of God.

I believe that as I continue to build my life upon the Word of God and press forward in my relationship with the Lord, I'm going to be supernaturally strengthened by the Holy Spirit. And as I get stronger in Him, more and more peace will pervade my life. The same is true for you.

> *Father God, I ask You to supernaturally strengthen my mind to stay focused on You so I can abide in Your peace. Father, You said that if I would ask anything according to Your will, You would do it. I know this is according to Your will, and I thank You in advance for causing Your peace to rule in my heart.*

Be Thankful

Every good thing given and every perfect gift is from above, coming down from the Father of lights, with whom there is no variation or shifting shadow.

—James 1:17

D O YOU REALIZE that thankfulness is a choice? I say that because we can choose what we will focus on. Some people look at life negatively and see the glass as half empty, while others see it as half full. The ones who see the glass as half full praise God for what He has given them, but those who see it as half empty look at that same glass and complain about what they lack.

I have observed this in my ministry to people. There are individuals in my congregation who are always telling me how much the messages have touched their lives. But there are others who have been in the congregation for years and have heard the same sermons yet have never once expressed any joy over the word. They have never said, "Oh, Rabbi, that sermon blessed me so much," or, "That word was just what I needed today."

Some people, it seems, are thankful even if they face challenges in life; others have an attitude of lack, and nothing is ever enough for them. The good news is that we can cultivate an attitude of thankfulness. James said every good and perfect gift comes from above. That means your life is a gift. The fact that you can read these words right now is a gift. Good health; the ability to walk; the ability to see, remember, and reason—these are all gifts coming down from the Father of lights. Too often we take these blessings for granted, not appreciating them until they're gone. We don't appreciate good health until we find ourselves sick. We don't appreciate our vision until it begins to fail. We don't appreciate our hearing capacities until they begin to diminish.

Beloved, let's thank God every day for what we have—the food that we eat, the home we live in, our friends and families. When we thank God for what we do have, He'll keep blessing us with more. So keep your eyes on Him, and choose to be thankful. Every breath we take is a gift from above.

> *Father God, help me to cultivate an attitude of gratitude. Help me to change my perspective so that I appreciate the blessings You have given me rather than focus on what I lack. Father God, help me to always be thankful.*

A Heart of Flesh

And I will give them one heart, and put a new spirit within them. And I will take the heart of stone out of their flesh and give them a heart of flesh.

—EZEKIEL 11:19

WHAT DOES THE Lord mean here when He says He's going to take out our hearts of stone and give us instead hearts of flesh? Think about this: Does a heart of stone feel anything? If you knock on a stone or pinch it or slam your fist down on it, will that stone feel anything? Absolutely not, right? But if you pinch or punch or knock on flesh, the flesh will feel it. So what the Lord is saying here is that He's going to take our hearts of stone that were previously insensitive to Him and unable to discern His Spirit, and He's going to give us instead hearts that will yield to His Spirit.

Beloved, God wants to help you become more and more sensitive to the Holy Spirit. Jesus said, "My sheep hear My voice, and I know them, and they follow Me" (John 10:27). Now, the ability to discern the voice of

God does not come overnight. It takes training. We don't hear His voice perfectly all at once. But if you'll make it your priority to know Him—to hear His voice and sense His Spirit working in your life—God is going to teach you to recognize His voice when He speaks. And you will be led into a deep relationship with God because He's given you the capacity to do so.

Father God, thank You for removing my old heart of stone and giving me a heart of flesh. Help me to be more sensitive to Your Spirit and to recognize Your voice when You are speaking. Lord, You said Your sheep hear Your voice, and I am one of Your sheep, so help me to not only discern Your leading but to trust what You are doing in my life. I want to partner with You to accomplish Your will in my life and in the earth.

Trust in the Lord

Blessed is the man who trusts in the LORD and whose trust is the LORD.

—JEREMIAH 17:7

CAN YOU IMAGINE how different our lives would be if we fully trusted the Lord? Burdens would be lifted because we would have such confidence in God, it would dispel our fears. Instead of thinking we are just victims of circumstance, we would realize that life isn't random and there is a reason for the things that happen.

Our lives would be transformed if we truly trusted God, but trust doesn't come naturally to us as human beings. Fortunately, however, it is something that can be developed. Trust grows as we deepen our knowledge of the Word of God and as the power of the Holy Spirit strengthens our inner man. And trust is refined as we go through tests in life.

Most people struggle to trust God because it is difficult to put our confidence in someone we can't see and feel. As we grow in our ability to trust God, we experience greater levels of freedom. You see, trusting the

Lord gives us a peace of mind that really can't come any other way. Nothing in the world has all the answers. Doctors don't have all the answers for our health. The world's economists don't have all the answers for our finances. Politicians don't have all the answers for the problems that plague our communities. The only way to truly have peace is by trusting in the Lord. That is why we should make it our goal in life to trust God more and more.

Beloved, I want to encourage you to be patient with yourself. But continue to do those things that will build trust in your life. Study God's Word, surrender to Him in obedience, and see what God does. As your trust increases, you're going to experience more internal happiness, and people are going see the power of God at work in your life.

Father God, strengthen me and help me to trust You. I know this world does not have all the answers, but You do. You hold my future in Your hands. Help me not to lean on my own understanding but to put my hope completely in You.

DAY 37

Marked by God's Power

When Israel saw the great power which the LORD had used against the Egyptians, the people feared the LORD, and they believed in the LORD and in His servant Moses.

—EXODUS 14:31

ONCE WHEN I was in Israel, I stood at the Red Sea and thought about a well-known account in the Bible. I know you are probably familiar with it. The Israelites had been slaves in Egypt for four hundred years, and after a mighty demonstration of God's power, Pharaoh let them go. Then Pharaoh changed his mind and sent his army to return them to slavery.

The Israelites were moving toward the land God promised them, but when they came up against the Red Sea, they found themselves trapped. With this sea in front of them and Pharaoh's army chasing them, they were facing an impossible situation. But God loved them so much that He did something supernatural. He parted the sea, enabling them to walk across on dry land.

From the ten plagues in Egypt to the parting of the Red Sea, the miracles God performed to bring the Israelites out of slavery and into the Promised Land marked His people. Exodus 14:31 says the people feared the Lord because of the mighty works He did, and they believed in Him.

Just as the supernatural power of God marked the Israelites, so too He is marking you. The Father is working supernaturally in the lives of His children, and the work He is doing in you will mark and change you. He may be delivering you from slavery to fear, anger, pride, or lust. Or maybe He is miraculously healing your body or restoring a broken relationship. Ask the Holy Spirit to bring you into a deeper revelation of His work in your life. As you turn your whole heart over to Him, He is marking you by His Spirit's power.

> *Father God, I ask that You break into my life with a mighty demonstration of Your power. Part any sea that needs to open in my life so I can walk in freedom and enter a deeper level of intimacy with You. Father, You've done powerful things for Your children in the past, and I ask, Abba Daddy, that You do those same types of things for me. May Your power mark me just as it marked the children of Israel.*

God Is Watching You

But without faith it is impossible to please Him,
for he who comes to God must believe that He is,
and that He is a rewarder of those who diligently
seek Him.

—Hebrews 11:6, NKJV

In order to please God, we must first believe that
He exists. We must believe that Jesus is alive and that
God is real. And then once we accept that God exists,
we must also believe He is a rewarder of those who diligently seek Him.

I want to encourage you today with this truth: God
is watching your every move. The Bible tells us that the
eyes of the Lord are running to and fro across the earth
looking for someone who will be fully devoted to Him
(2 Chron. 16:9). David said it was his endeavor to keep
the Lord continually before Him (Ps. 16:8). I want to
encourage you to cultivate an awareness of God's presence in your life, that His eyes are upon you. He is alive.
He is a God of love, and He is always aware of you.

God said to Jacob, "Behold, I am with you and will

keep you wherever you go" (Gen. 28:15). And to David the Lord said, "I will counsel you with My eye upon you" (Ps. 32:8).

Be aware that God is watching you right now. He's watching you every second of every day. He is not waiting for you to make a mistake so He can rain down judgment; He is looking for you to love Him with the same love with which He loves you. When you do, He will reward you—and the greatest reward of all is recognizing and experiencing the presence of God Himself in and around your life.

> *Father God, You are so worthy of my love and adoration. Thank You for this reminder that You are watching me and that You want me to come to You and fellowship with You and love You in return. Help me to seek You first.*

DAY 39

God Will Complete the Work

For I am confident of this very thing, that He who began a good work in you will perfect it until the day of Christ Jesus.

—PHILIPPIANS 1:6

GOD WILL COMPLETE the work He began in me, and He will do the same in you. No matter where you started or where you are in your walk with God, whether you are far along or not nearly where you hoped to be, you can look to the Father to complete within you what He started when you accepted Jesus as Messiah. He is in the process of conforming us to the image of His Son. He is making us like Jesus! "For those whom He foreknew, He also predestined to become conformed to the image of His Son, so that He would be the firstborn among many brethren" (Rom. 8:29).

The apostle Paul said He who began a good work in us would *perfect* it. Sometimes we feel condemned as Christians because we're holding ourselves to a standard of perfection that we can't seem to meet. I want you to understand that there is a difference between being perfect and being on a journey to perfection. You may feel as if you're failing right now because you're not "perfect," but if you're moving forward, if you're growing in God, then you're on the journey to perfection. If you are making progress toward becoming more like Jesus, you're successful.

God loves you. Trust Him to complete in you what He started. Just like a mom and dad love their baby who is stumbling as she's learning to walk, so does God keep loving you and me even when we fall. If there's something in your life that's weighing you down or that keeps tripping you up, give it to God. Keep talking to Him about it. Keep praying about it. Keep asking and asking and asking for help. The One who began the good work in you will complete it.

> *Father God, I love You today. I am so thankful that I can look to You to be the author and finisher of my faith. I thank You, Father God, that it's not up to me to perfect myself, but as I look to You and cling to You, You Yourself are working in and through me to perfect me and will complete what You started.*

Focus on God

Now may the God of hope fill you with all joy and peace in believing, so that you will abound in hope by the power of the Holy Spirit.

—ROMANS 15:13

A s YOU KNOW, the world around us is fallen and dark. Turn on the news, and you will hear about murder, disease, chaos, and war. There are terrorist threats of all kinds, and we hear of so many people around the world who are suffering.

Yet in Romans 15:13 our Father is described as the God of hope who wants us to have peace in believing by the power of the Holy Spirit. Think about the contrast between this God of hope who wants to fill us with joy and peace, and the darkness, sadness, and cynicism of this world. These are two completely different realities, which is why we need to be careful, beloved, to focus on God and not on the world.

We must *seize God's Word and not let anything else in*. If we are giving ourselves to the world all the time—feeding on the things of the world, taking counsel from people who don't look at life through the paradigm of God's Word, watching movies that entertain from a secular worldview—we are not going to have hope, we are not going to have peace, and we are not going to have joy.

But if we focus on God and magnify Him in our lives, if we feed on His Word, discipline our thoughts, and control what we look at and listen to, we will find ourselves growing in strength, peace, and the power of the Holy Spirit. It doesn't happen all at once, but it will happen. I promise you this: as you focus on God more and more, you will grow in peace, joy, and hope in Christ Jesus.

> *Father God, thank You for the wisdom to seize Your Word so I keep my eyes on You. Help me to feed my heart and mind with Your truth and not with the superficial, lying deceptions of the world. Thank You for being the God of hope who fills me with joy and peace by the power of Your Spirit.*

DAY 41

Choose to Praise

He brought me up out of the pit of destruction, out of the miry clay, and He set my feet upon a rock making my footsteps firm.

—PSALM 40:2

IT HAS BEEN almost forty years since I first came to faith in Jesus, and I know that if Jesus had not broken into my world, I surely would have been destroyed. Maybe you can relate. Even if you are not as far along in your Christian journey as you would like to be, you know that it is only because of Yeshua that you are where you are today. Where would you be without Him?

Reminding yourself of what God has done in your life is one of the most powerful things you can do as a believer in Jesus. Cultivating an attitude of gratitude gets your focus off your problems and on the One who saves. It gives you hope in the middle of life's storms as you think about what God has already done for you. He never changes. If God brought you through your last trial, He will bring you through this one too.

Some people think we praise God for His benefit. But

God does not need our praise. We need it. We need to remind ourselves of His love and goodness. Because God loves you, He saved you. He brought you up out of the pit of destruction and set your feet upon a rock. Do you really think He will abandon you now?

You may be going through a difficult time in your life. You might be facing marital difficulties or financial hardship or a health crisis. Whatever the situation, I want to challenge you to look at the big picture. Think about how far you've come and what would have happened if Jesus had not come into your life and redeemed you, and then choose to be thankful and trust Him now.

God uses life's challenges to make us stronger. So don't wallow in your current state. Give God glory. Rejoice and be thankful even in the midst of the trial because of what God has already done—He has brought you out of the pit and saved you from destruction.

> *Father God, I choose to praise and trust You even in the midst of my trials because You have already done so much for me. You saved me and brought me up out of the pit of destruction. Because You love me, I will spend eternity with You. Help me to cultivate an attitude of gratitude to bless and trust You at all times. Help me to not let my trials overshadow my consciousness of Your goodness toward me.*

DAY 42

We Are Overcomers

> Love never gives up, never loses faith, is always
> hopeful, and endures through every circumstance.
> —1 CORINTHIANS 13:7, NLT

GOD SAVED ME from defeat, and He did the same for
you. You see, when you are a child born of God's
love, you are a victor. The days of losing are behind you
because you are more than a conqueror in Christ Jesus.

Paul wrote in 1 Corinthians 13:7 that "love never
gives up…and endures through every circumstance."
Beloved, there is something in you that cannot die.
Jesus rose from the grave, He conquered death, He rose
through every power of darkness, and He sits now at
the right hand of the Father in complete victory—*and
He lives in you*. So you can't give up, because the One
who has overcome is inside you. In fact the Scripture
says he who is born of God overcomes the world (1 John
5:4). That makes you a winner!

No more thinking you are a loser. Renew your mind
with the Word of God. Lift up your head and see yourself seated at the right hand of God where Christ is

seated because the Scripture says you have been raised with Christ and are seated with Him in heavenly places (Eph. 2:6). You are not defeated, my friend. You are an overcomer in Jesus.

Father, You said that all authority in heaven and earth has been given unto You. Jesus, right now I come against every oppressive spirit that's making me look down and feel less than. I come against every demonic spirit of inferiority, and I speak freedom right now over my life in Yeshua's mighty name.

Don't Drink the Cup of Demons

You cannot drink the cup of the Lord and the
cup of demons; you cannot partake of the table
of the Lord and the table of demons.
—1 CORINTHIANS 10:21

WE DON'T ALWAYS realize that many of the things
we partake in have a spiritual aspect. You may
think it's just a TV show, just a movie, just a song, but
spirits operate through the media we consume.

When the Bible says, "You cannot drink the cup of the
Lord and the cup of demons," it is warning us against
compromising and leading double lives. But the forms
that compromise can take are not always overt. For
example, some people love God but also listen to music
celebrating things they know are wrong and watch movies
that accent sinful behaviors. When they do this, they are
drinking of the cup of demons, consuming what demons
are serving up, because anything that encourages a lifestyle contrary to the Word of God is not inspired by the
Spirit of God. It is energized by demons.

I want to encourage you, beloved, to practice fidelity

in your relationship with God. Be focused and refuse to compromise. This does not mean you are to become legalistic. My encouragement is that you not entertain yourself with things that dishonor Messiah Jesus or that encourage the sins Yeshua died to cleanse us of.

I know some churches focus so much on dos and don'ts that their members feel as if they are in bondage. That is not the heart of God. But there is no freedom in compromise, and it often leads to complete alienation from Jesus. This is why Yeshua warned us about being lukewarm, saying, "I know your deeds, that you are neither cold nor hot; I wish that you were cold or hot" (Rev. 3:15). The more we give our hearts to other lovers, the more we drift away from Him, and the weaker we become, until we are no longer effective witnesses for the kingdom.

I don't advocate simply following a bunch of rules; I encourage people to develop a relationship with Jesus, but we must guard that relationship. If your heart isn't focused on pleasing God, it can be lured to partake of the table of demons. God is asking us to deny ourselves and follow Him. We cannot drink of both His Spirit and the cup of demons. Let's not compromise. Messiah Jesus wants you to follow Him in the narrow way that leads to life.

> *Father, help me to guard against compromise.*
> *Awaken me supernaturally if my heart begins*
> *to drift away from You.*

DAY 44

Follow the Spirit's Leading

Boaz replied to her, "All that you have done for your mother-in-law after the death of your husband has been fully reported to me, and how you left your father and your mother and the land of your birth, and came to a people that you did not previously know. May the LORD reward your work, and your wages be full from the LORD, the God of Israel, under whose wings you have come to seek refuge."

—RUTH 2:11–12

IF YOU KNOW the biblical story of Ruth, you know she followed her mother-in-law, Naomi, into an unfamiliar land, where she ultimately fulfilled her destiny in the Lord. Not only did Ruth marry a wealthy landowner named Boaz, but she also gave birth to Obed, who became the grandfather of David, Israel's great king. Ruth's decision to leave everything she had known to embrace the God and people of Israel was so remarkable that she became one of only five women mentioned in Matthew's account of the genealogy of Jesus.

But do you know what? You and I are doing the same

thing. We are venturing out in life to follow the purposeful leading of the Ruach HaKodesh to fulfill our destiny in Him. And as we follow the Spirit of God, He will lead us into unfamiliar places and call us to take risks in faith, even as Ruth took a risk by leaving her people and joining herself to the nation of Israel.

Boaz took note of Ruth's courage and said, "May the Lord reward your work, and your wages be full from the Lord, the God of Israel, under whose wings you have come to seek refuge." I believe the Lord is speaking the same words to us today. As we follow the Holy Spirit's leading in our lives and seek refuge under His covering, we too will be rewarded.

So, beloved, let's take a lesson from Ruth and follow the leading of the Spirit of Elohim. As we do, we will be rewarded, and God will manifest His covering over us.

Father God, thank You for leading me by Your Ruach HaKodesh to fulfill my destiny in You. And thank You for being a rewarder of those who diligently seek You. Even as I go into unfamiliar territory, I will not fear, because You are with me. I trust You, Lord. Help me to yield fully to You and to find refuge under Your covering, as Ruth did.

Love in Deed

Let us not love with word or with tongue, but in deed and truth.

—1 John 3:18

I THINK IT'S GOOD to tell people that we love them and to do so often. But the Bible tells us in 1 John 3 that our love needs to go deeper than just words. There needs to be some kind of concrete action attached to our proclamations of love, behaviors that have substance to them.

There is a world full of people in need of love, which can make the call to love others seem overwhelming. So I think a great place to start is with those who are closest to us. We can love our families or our friends better. We can ask ourselves what we can do for them.

Now, think about this: When was the last time you did something for somebody just because you wanted to bless that person and not because there was something in it for you? Many times we do things for other people, but we are motivated by the way it will benefit us. That's not really love. Love is when we do something for somebody else not because there's something in it for us but simply because we want to bless that person. It's just that simple.

I believe we will begin to walk in the fullness of God's power when we really learn how to put other people first, when we really lead lives that are not just about meeting our own needs. We do need to have our own needs met, but the aim must go beyond just receiving for ourselves.

God wants us to be intentional about being a blessing to others. Yes, sometimes loving people with our words is exactly what God is calling us to do—to reach out and tell them how much we appreciate them. But sometimes our love needs to go beyond words and be demonstrated through concrete deeds. Whether by words or physical action, let's seek to grow in loving others.

Father, I ask You to strengthen me today by the Ruach HaKodesh, by the Holy Spirit. Impart life to me through Your Son by Your Spirit that I would share that love with others. I ask this, Father, in Yeshua's name.

Faith Involves Risk

Truly I say to you, if you have faith the size of
a mustard seed, you will say to this mountain,
"Move from here to there," and it will move; and
nothing will be impossible to you.

—MATTHEW 17:20

WE WANT TO see God move. We want to see miracles happen. We want the Lord to show up in
our lives. But many times miracles won't happen and
mountains won't move unless you and I exercise faith,
and that may involve taking a risk.

Let me give you an example of what I mean. One
year during Hanukkah, a woman attended services at
the congregation I lead in Toledo, Ohio. She had not
been able to attend for several months because she
had been in a wheelchair, and even on that night, she
couldn't stand up straight for even ten seconds without
falling. But she came to the service in the wheelchair
that Hanukkah night, and when I saw her, somehow I
just knew that her being in the wheelchair was of the
devil. I don't believe all sickness is a direct attack from

the devil, but I knew in my spirit that this woman being wheelchair bound was the work of Satan.

Faith rose up in my heart, and I went up to the woman in front of the entire congregation and said, "Silver and gold have I none, but what I have I give to thee. In the name of Jesus of Nazareth, get out of that wheelchair. Stand up and walk." The woman bounced out of that wheelchair and walked from one end of the sanctuary to the other, praising God!

For that miracle to have happened, I had to have faith. I had to take the risk of saying in front of everybody, "In the name of Jesus of Nazareth, stand up and walk." I could have been fearful and thought, "If nothing changes, I'll look like an idiot." But I didn't let pride or fear stop me from stepping out in faith.

Sometimes God is waiting for you to take action. I want to encourage you: don't just wait for God to show up. Exercise your faith because God moves through faith, and oftentimes walking in faith involves taking a risk.

Father God, Your Word says that if I have faith the size of a mustard seed, I will say to this mountain, "Move from here to there," and it will move; and nothing will be impossible to me. Holy Spirit, help me to walk in this level of faith. Let me not be hindered by fear or pride but have the courage to obey Your leading.

Revive Yourself in the Lord

My soul cleaves to the dust; revive me according
to Your word.

—PSALM 119:25

SOMETIMES WHEN I wake up after having a fitful
night's sleep, I think, "Wow, I don't feel like I slept
at all last night." And I wish I could just stay in bed.

But I have found that when I spend time with the
Lord, worshipping Him and reading His Word, my
soul supernaturally will begin to feel revived. Even if I
woke up feeling kind of down and sluggish, as I get into
God's Word, I am renewed.

David said in Psalm 119:25 that he was revived by the
Word of God, and that is absolutely what the Word does.
God's Word is "living and active and sharper than any
two-edged sword" (Heb. 4:12). It brings life to us. This is
why I always encourage people to spend time with God
first thing in the morning.

When we do this, we are practicing what I call the
Law of Firstfruits. This law challenges us to give God

our first and our best—whether it's the first of our finances, the first of our talents, or the first of our time.

You see, whenever the children of Israel had a harvest, they took the first of the yield and presented it to the Lord. And because they gave to God first, the rest of the harvest was considered sanctified. I believe that same principle is at work today. When we give the first part of our day to God upon waking up in the morning, the rest of the day becomes more blessed as a result.

Beloved, God's Word revives. So I challenge you to always give God the firstfruits of your day. Doing so will bring blessing to your life and revive your soul.

> *Father God, help me to give You my first and my best. Bless this day as I give You the first-fruits of my time. Help me to always seek You first because Your Word says that when I do, everything else will be added to me. Thank You, Father, for always being so good and gracious to me. Revive me today through Your Word. In Jesus' name, amen.*

The Best Is Yet to Come

Every man serves the good wine first, and when the people have drunk freely, then he serves the poorer wine; but you have kept the good wine until now.

—JOHN 2:10

THE FIRST MIRACLE Jesus performed was to turn water into wine at a wedding in Cana. When the guests drank the wine, they were surprised by how good it was. They said, "Most people serve the good wine first at a wedding, and then when everyone has drunk freely, they serve the bad wine. But in this case, you saved the best wine until last."

I see this story as an analogy for the lives of believers. Just as the latter wine Yeshua created was better than the former, so will the latter years of your life be better than the former. Why do I say this? It's because as you continue to seek Him, beloved, you are going to be changed from glory to glory and from grace to grace. You will just get better and better, stronger and stronger, and more and more like Jesus.

Day by day you are being changed. You are not the same person today that you were last year, and you are not going to be the same person a year from now that you are today. As you give your life to Jesus, as you continue to seek to obey Him, as you continue to give His Word preeminence in your life, as you continue to sit under sound teaching and apply it to your life, you are going to be supernaturally changed.

No matter how old you are or how long you have been following Messiah, keep believing that the best is yet to come.

> *Father God, I thank You that the best is yet to come. You are moving me from glory to glory and from strength to strength, and I declare that my latter years will be greater than my former years. Father, give me renewed hope, health, and vitality so I will remain strong for You even as I age. Thank You for changing me day by day as I seek You with my whole heart.*

Watch Over Your Heart

Watch over your heart with all diligence, for from it flow the springs of life.

—PROVERBS 4:23

MANY OF US unfortunately live from the outside in rather than from the inside out. We are aware of what people are saying about us and how we look to the world, but we do not know what is happening in our own hearts and minds. We are out of touch with what the Spirit of God is doing inside of us, causing us to lack the discernment we need in order to overcome.

To overcome, you must become conscious of what is going on in your mind. Thoughts of worry, fear, and other things that are not rooted in the truth can begin to control you if you do not take authority over them. And you cannot take authority over something you do not realize is operating in your life.

This is why you must watch over your heart and your thoughts. When you recognize that something in your heart or in your thinking is not in line with the truth or is not pleasing to God, you must address it immediately before it has a chance to do further damage. If you have ever dealt with weeds in your lawn, you know if you don't pull them when you begin to see them grow, they will spread and begin to destroy the healthy plants.

Ungodly thoughts and beliefs are the same way. If you let them go unchecked, they will continue to grow and choke out more and more of the truth you have received until you can barely remember how deeply the Father loves you. Then the enemy's lies will begin to resonate as truth. And when you come into agreement with the enemy by believing the lies he tells you, you give him authority to control you with fear, hopelessness, and despair.

Beloved, pay attention to your heart. Notice what you are thinking. When you see yourself going down a path that is not of God, stop and confess your sins or wrong thinking to the Lord. If you ask the Father to help you reorient your attitude and thoughts, He will bring your heart into harmony with Himself.

> *Holy Spirit, come and break into my heart, break into my thoughts, and bring them into order so my life can be pleasing to You. Make me sensitive to what I am thinking and feeling so I will not give the enemy a foothold in my life. I pray that the meditations of my heart would be acceptable in Your sight, O Lord, my Rock and my Redeemer.*

Treasure the Word

My son, give attention to my words; incline your ear to my sayings. Do not let them depart from your sight; keep them in the midst of your heart. For they are life to those who find them and health to all their body.

—PROVERBS 4:20–22

WHEN WE RECEIVE God's wisdom, when we receive His words, whether they're spoken through the pages of Scripture or to our hearts through the Holy Spirit, we need to treasure that word and cling to it.

This is why I believe it is important that we write down the revelation we receive. When God begins to speak to me about a certain thing, I will write it down because I find that if I don't write it down, if I don't cling to it, if I don't treasure it in my heart, I have a tendency to forget about it.

That is just human nature. Life goes on, and we begin to think about other things. So when you receive the word of God, and it really strikes you, I believe it is important that you write it down. Then go back every so often and review the truths God has revealed to you. By doing this, you will be able to move forward in the truth He is imparting to you more fully and effectively.

Beloved, don't let the Word of God roll off your back. Take hold of it.

> *Father God, I treasure Your Word. I hide it in my heart that I might not sin against You. Bring to my remembrance the things You have spoken, whether through Scripture or through Your Spirit. Let Your Word lead me into a deeper revelation of who You are, how much You love me, and my role in shining the light of truth in a lost and dying world.*

You Are a Victor in Him

You are from God, little children, and have overcome them; because greater is He who is in you
than he who is in the world.

—1 John 4:4

It has been almost forty years since Jesus revealed
Himself to me. At that time in my life, I was on the
verge of being snuffed out by the enemy. I can't even
imagine what would have happened if Jesus hadn't
come to me and delivered me.

Not long after I accepted Yeshua as Messiah, I started
reading the Word of God and I read 1 John 4:4. The
idea that I had overcome the world was revolutionary. It
changed my life and empowered me. It saved me from
looking down and feeling defeated to looking up and
ascending in power into victory.

Obviously this was a process. I had to fight through
opposition, and so will you. But no matter how difficult
the fight, because you are in Jesus, you are an overcomer,
and you are on the road to progressive victory. You are
going from strength to strength, from grace to grace,

from faith to faith, and from glory to glory. Greater is He who is in you, beloved, than he who is in the world.

Stop looking to the world to affirm you. The world is a hostile place. The Scriptures say the world lies in darkness. Your victory is not going to come from people affirming you. Your victory comes when you get in touch with the fact that the One who has overcome lives inside you, and because you are born again, you are a victor in Him.

Father God, thank You for giving me victory by Your Spirit. Help me to look to You and seek the applause of heaven over the applause of men. Help me look to You for victory in all my circumstances and remember that I am an overcomer in You.

Real Friendship

A man of too many friends comes to ruin, but there is a friend who sticks closer than a brother.
—PROVERBS 18:24

IN THIS FACEBOOK generation where people are collecting friends, it has become easy to develop superficial relationships. So many of the "friends" that crowd our social media accounts are not friends at all; they are just props to prove our popularity.

This social media trend runs counter to the wisdom of the Word of God. The Bible doesn't tell us to count friends, to see how many connections we can add to our Facebook page just so it appears to the world that we are "somebody." Rather, God's Word places great value on friends who can really be trusted.

"There is a friend," the Word says, "who sticks closer than a brother" (Prov. 18:24). Think about this: Have you been pursuing friends just so you can appear to be important in the world's eyes? Or are you trying to develop real relationships with people who have integrity and will be there for you when you need them? It is better to have a few good friends than to have 150 superficial relationships.

Beloved, let us preserve and continue to build key relationships throughout our days with the people whom God has called us to walk with as true friends. The Lord puts value not on the number of friends we have but on the quality of the friendships. All true relationships require sacrificial love, compassion, patience, and forgiveness.

And if you desire to make new friends, reach out strategically and be willing to make the first move. There is nothing wrong with being proactive in developing new relationships. Just pursue friendships that really matter.

Father God, thank You for being a friend who sticks closer than a brother and for putting people in my life who love me. Father, I ask that You help me to appreciate the friends You have placed in my life and not seek after superficial connections. Help me to develop friendships with the people You want in my life so we can grow together and support one another.

DAY 53

Trust God's Love

There is no fear in love; but perfect love casteth out fear: because fear hath torment. He that feareth is not made perfect in love.

—1 JOHN 4:18, KJV

THE DEVIL ATTACKS God's people from many angles, but I think his primary way of tormenting us is fear. We fear not having enough money, fear not being loved, fear sickness, fear growing old, fear being in a car wreck, fear losing our homes or our jobs or our businesses—the list goes on and on.

Fear torments, but the Bible says that "perfect love casteth out fear" (1 John 4:18, KJV). I believe this means that when we understand experientially that we are loved by the Father, we will not live in fear. In other words, when we have truly received in our hearts, minds, and emotions that we are perfectly cherished by the Father and that we can trust Him to take care of us because He loves us, we will not be afraid.

If we truly believe Father God is committed to us because He cherishes us so deeply and that He'll do what He promised He would do—which is to supply all our needs according to His riches in glory (Phil. 4:19)—then we're not going to be afraid of running out of money. We're not going to be afraid of being alone or of growing old because we will believe His Word when He said, "I will be your God throughout your lifetime—until your hair is white with age. I made you, and I will care for you. I will carry you along and save you" (Isa. 46:4, NLT).

Lift your heart and thoughts today to trust the faithfulness of God's love for you. Know this, beloved one: if you belong to Jesus, He is going to see you through to the end. Father God is always watching over you. He has numbered each hair on your head. Do not be afraid. Father is going to take care of you and meet all your needs, even unto the very end. You can trust His love. Yeshua promised and said, "I will never leave you nor forsake you" (Heb. 13:5, NKJV).

> *Father God, help me to trust Your love. When I am afraid or when I am facing hardships in life, help me to remember that I have overcome the world in You.*

Discipline Is a Blessing

For His anger is but for a moment, His favor is for a lifetime; weeping may last for the night, but a shout of joy comes in the morning.

—PSALM 30:5

SOMETIMES BECAUSE OF the Father's love for us, He will discipline us. The Bible tells us that the Father disciplines every son and daughter He receives and that no discipline feels good when we're going through it, but the end result is peace (Heb. 12:4–11). Discipline is painful for a relatively short time, but the joy that comes afterward lasts a lifetime.

It is a beautiful thing that our Father loves us so much that He will discipline us. I personally find a great deal of security in this. I actually pray for His discipline because even though it may hurt for a little while, it will keep me on the straight and narrow path that leads to blessing. I would rather that than for the Father not to discipline me and I end up going astray without even knowing it and then find myself lost, ruined, and broken in life.

So you see, beloved, the discipline of the Lord is a gift. We should pray for it. We should thank God for it. We should love Him for it. The pain of His discipline lasts just for a little while, but joy and peace come in the morning and last for a lifetime. I wouldn't trade that for anything. Would you?

Father God, I thank You for Your discipline because Your Word says that You discipline those You love. Help me to never view Your correction as a bad thing, but adjust my perspective so I see it as the gift that it is.

Do Something

Is anyone among you suffering? Then he must pray. Is anyone cheerful? He is to sing praises.
—JAMES 5:13

YOU AND I must act. James 5:13 says, "Is anyone among you suffering? Then he must pray. Is anyone cheerful? He is to sing praises." James is telling us that to live in the power of God and experience the momentum of the Holy Spirit, we must act. Are you suffering? Don't just sit there and let the enemy beat you up. James says to pray. If God is doing great things in your life and you're feeling cheerful, sing His praises. Whether our circumstances are good or bad, we are not to be passive. We are to do something.

Too many people are waiting for God to do everything. They do not understand that the upper world is connected to the lower world. It is not just what God does in the upper world that affects our reality; it also matters what we do here in the lower world. Even as God activates us from the upper world, we can also move God to action here in the lower world by seeking

Him in prayer and by praising Him. This is why the Lord said in James 4:8, "Draw near to Me, and I will draw near to you" (author's paraphrase).

You see, when we draw near to God, we are doing something in the lower world, and He responds from the upper world and draws near to us. There is a partnership between us and God. We can't just be passive and then wonder why God is not moving in our situation. We need to act as well. God is looking for us to partner with Him.

I want to say to you, beloved one: don't be flaccid in your walk with God. Declare your love for Him in word and in deed. Praise Him. Talk to Him. He loves you, and He is just waiting for you to love Him back. When you do, He will respond.

> *Father God, awaken my heart to the reality of my responsibility. Help me to not be passive but to partner with You to bring supernatural change in my life and in the lives of others. I commit to seeking You in prayer when trials come and to praise You in the good times. I desire to always move toward You. I love You, Lord.*

Be a Priest of God

And He said to them, "Go into all the world and preach the gospel to all creation."

—MARK 16:15

THE MANDATE TO go out and reproduce is for every Christian. It is not an assignment reserved for a specific group of people. All believers are called to lead people to faith, and once a person comes to know Jesus, that individual has a responsibility to lead others to Him. This is how the church will go into the world and preach the gospel to all creation.

Accepting the mandate to share your faith is going to separate you from some people, but that is what it means to be holy—to be separate and unique. God has called those who follow Him a peculiar people, a chosen race, a royal priesthood (1 Pet. 2:9). I want you to particularly focus on Peter's admonition that we are a *royal* priesthood.

In the Old Testament a priest did three primary things: draw near to God, offer sacrifices to the Lord, and impart the grace to the people. People living apart from Jesus need us to take this mandate seriously and be a priest of God. The world needs us to draw near to God for ourselves, offer Him the sacrifice of our own bodies, and then minister the things of the kingdom to others. God is pleased when we do this, for we are working on His behalf.

Father, I accept my responsibility to be a priest of God. Show me how I can share my faith with those around me so Your Word will spread and everyone will hear it.

God Hears

It will also come to pass that before they call, I will answer; and while they are still speaking, I will hear.

—ISAIAH 65:24

NO MATTER HOW faint our cries may be, God always hears us. This is such an amazing truth. Prayer is simply reaching out to God; it can be the loudest shout or the softest whisper. Whether you reach out to Him in your heart, in your mind, or with your voice raised, He hears it all.

First Peter 3:12 says, "For the eyes of the Lord are toward the righteous, and His ears attend to their prayer." Whenever we call upon Him, He answers, but we must be seeking to live in a way that is pleasing to Him. We must choose to live righteously.

That doesn't mean we have to be perfect. If we had to be perfect, no one would be able to talk to God, because we all have sinned and fallen short of God's standards. God understands that we are not perfect and has compassion on us, but He does expect us to be on a journey in Him to perfection. We just need a big yes in our hearts. We just need to be putting one foot in front of the other every day, moving forward in our relationship with God, being quick to repent when we do something wrong, and steadily conquering the darkness and the flesh that want to overwhelm and control our lives. As long as you are making progress, you are a success.

God hears you, beloved. So take heart. God loves you, He is listening, and He will answer when you call out to Him.

> *Father God, thank You for hearing me, whether I shout or whisper. Father, may I never doubt that You not only hear but also will answer my prayers.*

Resistance Training

No temptation has overtaken you but such as is common to man; and God is faithful, who will not allow you to be tempted beyond what you are able, but with the temptation will provide the way of escape also, so that you will be able to endure it.

—1 Corinthians 10:13

WE ARE CONSTANTLY bombarded with temptations to satisfy the lusts of the flesh. The images we see, the thoughts that come into our heads, the materialism that surrounds us—they all appeal to our natural desires. But the Lord tells us to resist temptation. Some people wonder why they can't just become immune to temptations, why they have to constantly fight. I want you to know, beloved one, that God uses temptation to do something powerful in your life. As you resist temptation, you become stronger.

Know that God is going to get you through the temptation and give you victory. He is going to bring you to the other side of the mountain, but it is important that you resist, because as you do, you get stronger. Think about bodybuilders. How do they build such muscles? Through what is called resistance training. They push their muscles against weight, and as their muscles are being resisted by the weight, their muscles are being built up.

God actually uses temptation in our lives to make us powerful. In the Gospels of Matthew and Luke, the first thing that God did in Jesus' life after He was baptized in the Jordan River was lead Him into the wilderness to be tempted. Think about that. Right after God said, "This is My beloved Son, in whom I am well-pleased" (Matt. 3:17), He led Yeshua into a place of temptation. And what happened as a result? Yeshua came out of that experience in the power of the Spirit and began ministering throughout the region (Luke 4:14).

All of us will experience temptation. I want to encourage you to resist it because God is going to make you strong as you do so. It may take time, but you are going to get the victory, you are going to get tough, and you are going to get happy and free. Resist in Jesus' name.

> *Father God, I thank You that no matter what temptation I face, You will provide the way of escape so I will be able to endure it. And I thank You that You are using those times to make me stronger. Cause me to grow in the power of Your Spirit as I resist the darkness.*

DAY 59

Receive God's Word

He who is of God hears the words of God.

—John 8:47

You may remember that in John 10:27 Yeshua said, "My sheep hear My voice." But the truth is oftentimes thoughts come into our mind, and we're not sure if they are from God. That does not mean this scripture is not true. I have found that as we grow in experience with God, we are better and better able to discern what is His voice and what is not. We grow through experience, and Scripture says that through maturity, we gain the ability to discern between good and evil (Heb. 5:14).

But in John 8:47, when Jesus said, "He who is of God hears the words of God," He wasn't just pointing to a person who hears the Word; He was describing an individual who is willing to receive and act on God's Word. Many times people read the Scriptures, but they are not willing to receive what the Bible says. For instance, Jesus said, "I am the way, and the truth, and the life; no one comes to the Father but through Me" (John 14:6). He who is of God will not only hear that but also

120

receive it. That person will come to Christ and say, "Yes, Jesus, I want to know and love You." But he who is not of God and does not want to come into agreement with the authority of God will not receive that Word. Instead, that person will agree with some man-made, politically correct, false form of spirituality that basically says, "All paths lead to the same place. Who are Christians to say that their God is the only way to heaven?"

"He who is of God," Jesus said, "hears the words of God." But to be able to hear God's words, we need to want to receive His Word, and this is a gift from God. The Bible says, "We love Him because He first loved us" (1 John 4:19, NKJV). So if you are one who loves and receives God's words, it is because God put a supernatural love for Him in your heart. The hungrier you are to receive His Word, the better you will hear Him, and the better you hear Him, the more you will experience Him. And as you draw closer to God, you will become better able to discern His voice.

> *Father God, give me a supernatural love for Your Word. Like David did, let me long to hear Your voice speaking into my life. Move in my heart so that I will receive Your truth and hear Your voice more clearly.*

Flee Those Things

But flee from these things, you man of God, and
pursue righteousness, godliness, faith, love, perseverance and gentleness.

—1 TIMOTHY 6:11

To DENY THE flesh is a hard thing. That is why the
apostle Paul told his protégé Timothy to flee from
unrighteousness. You cannot play with fire and not get
burned, so Paul told Timothy to not even get close but
instead to run from the danger.

There is wisdom in not putting yourself in a position
where you will be tempted to compromise. First Timothy
6:11 is saying that if you are struggling in your life, perhaps attracted to something you shouldn't be drawn to,
you need to flee that thing. Don't say, "Well, I'm going
to use moderation." Flee from it and instead pursue the
things of God—righteousness, love, faith, and godliness.

We transform our own souls by denying ourselves
the things of the flesh and choosing instead the things
of the Spirit. You see, Galatians 5:17 reveals a spiritual
law: "The flesh lusteth against the Spirit, and the Spirit

against the flesh: and these are contrary the one to the other: so that ye cannot do the things that ye would" (KJV). The Bible says if we yield to the flesh, we're going to reap destruction. But if we overcome the flesh and pursue instead the spirit of love, gentleness, peace, joy, etc., we are going to reap eternal life. (See Galatians 6:8.)

I want to charge you today to remember you are in a fight and you cannot yield to the flesh. You have to flee the things of the flesh and pursue the fruit of the Spirit. We can't put ourselves in positions where we are likely to compromise. For example, if you have a problem with alcohol, don't even consider having a drink. If you struggle with sexual temptation, run from situations where you could be entangled.

When you practice this principle of denying the flesh, you are going to reap life, and as you age, your life will be filled with contentment and peace. God said, "I have set before you life and death, the blessing and the curse. So choose life in order that you may live" (Deut. 30:19). Choose life. Flee the temptations of the flesh.

> *Father God, thank You for making a way of escape for me when I am tempted. Help me to run from danger and not entertain it. Help me to pursue Your will instead of the lust of the flesh, and let the fruit of Your Spirit be made manifest in my life.*

Keep Speaking the Truth

And even if our gospel is veiled, it is veiled to those who are perishing, in whose case the god of this world has blinded the minds of the unbelieving so that they might not see the light of the gospel of the glory of Christ, who is the image of God.

—2 CORINTHIANS 4:3–4

WHEN WE SHARE our faith with people and they reject it, oftentimes in the natural we feel as though they are rejecting us. Sometimes people are hostile when we share truth with them. When we share moral standards with a world that is in opposition to God's authority, we will experience blowback. When we talk about Jesus being the only way, when we talk about marriage being between a man and a woman, or when we talk about the gospel itself, we will at times get hostile reactions. When that happens, we can be tempted to take the rejection and the hostility personally. But I want to remind you that they are not rejecting you. Rather, their minds have been blinded by the god of this world.

Be encouraged, beloved. People will reject us. Jesus

said, "If they persecuted Me, they will persecute you, because the student is not greater than his teacher. I am the teacher. If they rejected Me, they are going to reject you too." (See Matthew 10:24–25 and John 15:20.) But remember, Jesus also said, "Blessed are those who are persecuted for righteousness' sake, for theirs is the kingdom of heaven" (Matt. 5:10, NKJV).

I want to inspire you to keep on speaking the truth in love. Keep on being bold. Keep on lifting up God's standards to the world because we have been called to be lights and truth bearers in the earth. The Lord told His disciples to go out and preach the gospel, to share the truth, and if the people receive the word, stay there. But if they reject it, shake the dust off your feet and go on to the next town. (See Matthew 10:5–15.)

It is the same way when we are sharing with individuals today. When sharing Messiah Jesus with a person who is interested, keep speaking the truth. But if someone is rejecting the message, move on to the next person. Jesus said, "You are the light of the world. A city set on a hill cannot be hidden; nor does anyone light a lamp and put it under a basket, but on the lampstand, and it gives light to all who are in the house" (Matt. 5:14–15).

Father God, I thank You for the courage and boldness to always stand for You. Help me to not fear rejection but to keep speaking the truth.

The Anointing Breaks the Yoke

So it will be in that day, that his burden will be removed from your shoulders and his yoke from your neck, and the yoke will be broken because of fatness.

—ISAIAH 10:27

W E HAVE ALL at one time or another felt weighed down by something, as if a burden is around our neck or on our shoulders pressing down on us. This is a picture of the yoke of oppression the prophet was referring to in Isaiah 10:27. That yoke may be fear, worry, or depression. It may be something you have been dealing with so long that you think it will never go away. But Isaiah 10:27 gives us hope.

The verse says the yoke is broken because of fatness, or "because of the anointing," as the King James Version puts it. In other words, the fatness is the anointing, and the anointing breaks the yoke of oppression. Now consider the fact that 1 John 2:20 says you have received an anointing from the Holy One. This is not the anointing on your pastor or on your prayer partner. John is saying *you* are anointed. That means you have what you need to break free of everything in your life that is keeping you bound.

Jesus wants you to be free. You have to believe that. Jesus said, "If you continue in My word, then you are truly disciples of Mine; and you will know the truth, and the truth will make you free" (John 8:31–32). Beloved, you were created and saved to stand up and break every yoke that is preventing the Spirit of God from being fully manifest through your life. Don't stop a quarter of the way up the mountain. Continue on to the top of the mountain.

God wants to break every yoke off our lives by His anointing. The Bible says Jesus has come to make us free (Gal. 5:1), and "where the Spirit of the Lord is, there is liberty" (2 Cor. 3:17). I pray that you will believe this and that you will set your mind to overcome in this world. Freedom and liberty are your portion. Don't settle for anything less. Keep on pressing in and pressing on. It often happens little by little, but you are being changed day by day. Keep your eyes set on Jesus.

> *Father God, help me to stand boldly in the truth that I can be free of every yoke of bondage. I declare that I am anointed, and I resist every device of the enemy to keep me bound by oppression. I declare freedom over my life in the name of Messiah Jesus.*

Have Confidence in God's Love

Therefore the LORD longs to be gracious to you, and therefore He waits on high to have compassion on you.

—ISAIAH 30:18

BELOVED, WE LIVE in a culture today that is so experientially based that people often do not spend the time to grow deep roots in the Word of God. So as soon as their circumstances or experiences change, they struggle in their faith and wonder if God really cares about them. This is why we need more than just an emotional experience with God. We cannot be satisfied with just going to church for a touch from the Father; we must root ourselves in His Word so we can walk in the light of the truth even when we don't feel anything emotionally.

Sometimes when we face challenges in life, we can begin to think God has abandoned or forgotten us. Some people are even afraid of God, thinking He is mad at them and is going to pour out His wrath on them and send them to hell. But Isaiah 30:18 says the Lord longs to be gracious to us. God is tenderhearted. The enemy, Satan, is called the accuser of the brethren (Rev. 12:10). But God does not accuse us. God is gracious. He loves us. If we could have saved ourselves, Jesus would not have had to come. But Father God had mercy on us. He looks at us with compassion, and He is just waiting for us to reach out to Him in confidence that He loves us.

I want you to know that Jesus died for you because the Father loves you and wants to bring you close to Himself. Reach out to God today in confidence that He loves you.

> *Father God, in Yeshua's name I take authority over all forms of demonic oppression that would keep me from having confidence in Your love for me. I reject every lie that is telling me You are mad at me when in fact You love me and long to be gracious to me. You wait on high to have compassion on me. I will walk in the truth of Your Word and not let my emotions dictate what I believe about Your love for me.*

DAY 64

You Belong to God

For if we have become united with Him in the likeness of His death, certainly we shall also be in the likeness of His resurrection, knowing this, that our old self was crucified with Him, in order that our body of sin might be done away with, so that we would no longer be slaves to sin.

—ROMANS 6:5–6

IF YOU KNOW the Lord, you should consider yourself dead to a life of sin. Whatever sinful habits you had before knowing Jesus, whatever dark thought patterns you had before you came to faith in Christ, whatever addictions you had before you were saved—you need to consider yourself dead to or released from those things.

Now, the truth is that our bodies still have appetites. There are certain bodily desires that do not just go away because we are saved. Sexual temptation, for instance, does not just go away, because it is a natural by-product of being human. But we are to consider ourselves dead to illicit sexual experiences, crucifying such desires by the power of the Spirit.

I believe the Lord is telling us through this passage in Romans 6 that even as Jesus was raised to newness of life after being crucified, we also have been released from the old life we lived before we chose to follow Him, and we too have been raised to a new life that is dedicated and alive to God. This means our lives are not our own. If we truly believe Jesus saved and purchased us by His blood, then we will recognize that we are God's possession. We don't belong to ourselves. We belong to the One who lived and died and rose again on our behalf. And because we belong to Him, we need to choose Him—to choose what is right and crucify the deeds of our flesh.

Beloved, the old life is passed away. We are dead to that life. We have been raised to newness of life. Now we must choose Jesus and put the power of darkness under our feet. It is a fight, but the joy of the battle is that there is a great reward for those who war and win. Revelation 2:7 tells us that those who overcome will "eat of the tree of life which is in the Paradise of God."

> *Father God, I believe that You purchased my salvation by Your blood, and I am Yours. I choose to live for You and crucify the deeds of the flesh. My old life has passed away, and I have been raised to a new life in You. Thank You for setting me free from bondage to sin.*

DAY 65

Fresh Strength

Yet those who wait for the LORD will gain new strength; they will mount up with wings like eagles, they will run and not get tired, they will walk and not become weary.

—ISAIAH 40:31

THERE HAVE BEEN times in my life when I just felt tired, as if I had no strength at all. I was so weary that I felt if God did not step in, I would sink. Have you ever felt that way? But Isaiah 40:31 gives us the confidence that if we just curl up in the Lord and hibernate there somehow, God will supernaturally impart new strength to our hearts, and as Isaiah 40:31 says, we will rise up again.

If you find yourself in a season when you have just run out of strength or of faith, and you feel you cannot go on, know this: you are not going to sink. Trust and believe that God is going to come to you again and rejuvenate you—that He is going to impart fresh strength and new revelation to you. He will be faithful to do so every single time.

So don't panic when you go through those times of weariness or doubt. Don't panic if you feel lost and as if you cannot go on. Father God is still holding you in His everlasting arms, and this scripture that Isaiah gave us thousands of years ago will be proven true in your life once again. You will mount up with wings like eagles. You will run and not get tired. You will walk and not become weary. In other words, God is going to refresh and revitalize you. He is going to be faithful to you, beloved. He is going to see you through to the end, and though you may stumble, because of Jesus you will never fall.

Father God, thank You for renewing my strength. You cause me to mount up with wings like eagles, to run and not get tired, and to walk and not become faint. Lord, I trust that You will see me through to the end and fill me afresh with Your Spirit.

His Gentleness Makes Us Great

You have also given me the shield of Your salvation, and Your right hand upholds me; and Your gentleness makes me great.

—Psalm 18:35

DAVID SAID THAT Father God's gentleness made him great, and oh, how true that is in the lives of His chosen ones. We are continually falling short of perfection, but the Father loves us so much, and He is so gentle toward us. He doesn't judge us for not being perfect; He just keeps helping and strengthening us.

A parent doesn't get mad or condemn an infant when the baby falls as he is attempting to walk. The parent keeps on loving the baby, encouraging and supporting the child. As time goes by, that baby gets stronger and stronger until he eventually begins to walk without losing his balance. Beloved, this is the same way Father God loves you and me. Micah 7:19 says, "He will again have compassion on us." I want you to know that God's mercy never fails. If you know Him, love Him, and have been chosen by Him, God's faithfulness will never fail you.

When I look at my own life and see how kind and gracious God has been to me, it just melts my heart. If the Father had not saved and called me, my life would have ended in destruction. But God's gentleness makes us great. How often have you looked back on your life and considered the wrong thoughts you had or the words you spoke in frustration or anger? Perhaps it wasn't what you did but what you didn't do, such as lacking gratitude. Through it all the Father has continued to love and be gracious to you, and He will never stop.

I recently talked to a friend, and when I asked him how he was, he said, "Father God has been ridiculously gracious to me." I love that expression because it is so true. God has been ridiculously gracious to us as He has poured out His lovingkindness on us.

God loves you. Run strong in His love.

> *Father God, I want to love You in a way that is worthy of who You are. Father, I ask You today to help me love You like Jesus loves You, because You said as He is, so also now are we (1 John 4:17). Father, thank You so much for loving me and being so ridiculously gracious to me.*

God Has Something New for You

Do not call to mind the former things, or ponder things of the past. Behold, I will do something new, now it will spring forth; will you not be aware of it? I will even make a roadway in the wilderness, rivers in the desert.

—ISAIAH 43:18–19

GOD IS ALWAYS doing a new thing. Only dead things don't change. Anything that is alive is constantly changing.

We need to always be looking for the new thing because the Spirit of God lives in us. The Ruach HaKodesh, which can be translated to mean the holy breath, or wind of God, is always fresh and is in continuous motion. His movement is never mechanical; the Spirit of God is constantly bubbling up from within us and bringing new life.

This is why when you abide in Jesus, when you abide in the vine, you can expect new things to manifest in and around your life. You can expect to experience new dimensions of God's presence and fresh emanations of His Spirit. God is creative, and He can do things beyond anything you and I can ask or think.

So I want to encourage you to never stop expecting God to do something new, even until your last days on this earth. Keep believing that God has something new for you. And when He brings the new thing, embrace it. Second Corinthians 3:18 declares that we "are being transformed...from glory to glory." Change is part of growing in God. So even if it is uncomfortable or unfamiliar, always stay open to the new.

> *Father God, I thank You for doing a new thing in my life. You are the Creator, and You are continually creating something brand-new in me. Raise my expectations, Father, that You will bring new life, new songs, new creativity, new dreams and visions. May I never fear change but always embrace the new thing You are doing in my life.*

DAY 68

Because of Jesus

The angel said to the women, "Do not be afraid; for I know that you are looking for Jesus who has been crucified. He is not here, for He has risen, just as He said."

—MATTHEW 28:5–6

THERE ARE TWO traditional sites in Israel that Christian tourists usually visit to remember Yeshua's resurrection: the Church of the Holy Sepulchre, which was built on the site where some people believe Jesus was crucified and buried, and the Garden Tomb, which others believe is an authentic site. Whether either of these places is exactly where Yeshua died, was buried, or rose from the dead is not important to me. What is important is that He did rise from the dead.

The fact of Yeshua's resurrection is what our whole faith is built on. If Jesus had not risen from the dead, then we would still be dead in our trespasses and sins. God the Father raising Yeshua from the dead was the proof that God accepted Yeshua's death on the cross as His provision for the forgiveness of sin.

The angel said in Matthew 28:6, "Why are you looking for Him? He has risen." Paul named individuals that Yeshua appeared to after he rose from the dead, five hundred of whom were still alive at the time of Paul's writing (1 Cor. 15:5–6). Beloved, the resurrection of the Lord Jesus Christ is no fairy tale. Yeshua rose from the dead and is now seated at the right hand of the Father. And because Yeshua triumphed over death, we too have power and victory in His name.

I want you to know that because of Yeshua, you are an overcomer. Because of Messiah Jesus, you win!

King Jesus, thank You for securing my victory over sin, death, hell, and the grave through Your death and resurrection. You are so great and greatly to be praised. Because You triumphed on the cross, I can overcome every form of demonic bondage that would seek to thwart my destiny. I claim that victory right now.

Don't Waste Your Trial

> Blessed is a man who perseveres under trial; for once he has been approved, he will receive the crown of life which the Lord has promised to those who love Him.
>
> —JAMES 1:12

JAMES TELLS US we need to persevere when we are under trial. This means we need to hold on to the Lord and listen through times of testing so we will handle the trial correctly. The Bible also tells us that we shouldn't act as if something strange is happening to us when we encounter various difficulties in life (1 Pet. 4:12). As we encounter these various trials and hang on to the Lord through them and choose correctly through them, our faith is being refined in the fire so it will come out as pure gold.

Everything you face is an opportunity for refining. So don't waste your trial! In other words, when you're about to lose your temper, when you're about to say something harsh, hold yourself in the peace of God. Maintain a disciplined mind. Continue to abide in Him.

Don't let the frustration take you off course. Don't be drawn out of the Lord's truth.

When we persevere under trial, God establishes us in Him. We become mature in Christ; we are filled afresh with the Spirit of God. We move deeper into the fullness of Jesus Himself, and there is a reward at the other end of that journey: we become more like Yeshua.

This is why when we are facing a trial, we should literally thank God for it because if we handle the trial correctly, it is going to conform us to the image of Messiah Jesus. We're going to be brought into a place of peace and maturity. We're going to ascend out of darkness into His marvelous light, and we are going to be rewarded for our perseverance.

Life is a challenge. It is filled with trials, but the Bible says he who overcomes will inherit the paradise of God (Rev. 2:7). Choose rightly, beloved. Don't waste your trials.

> *Father God, Your Word declares that the testing of my faith builds perseverance. Help me not to give up in the midst of trials but to run to You, hang on to You, lean on You, and seek You for strength.*

True Faith Is Active

> For just as the body without the spirit is dead, so also faith without works is dead.
>
> —James 2:26

REAL FAITH IS living and moving. Even as the spirit brings life to the body, true faith brings life to our spirits and causes us to act. We live in a generation today that is so focused on grace that sometimes people are not willing to assume the responsibility that comes with grace. The fact is true grace produces faith, and true faith produces works.

We are not saved by works, but we are known by our works. We cannot just believe God when we are in church raising our hands during worship. True faith is evident in the choices we make each day. Our faith should change us, and that transformation should be evident. If we truly believe God, we should look and act differently than we once did. We should be alive for Jesus and in passionate pursuit of Him.

True faith does not make us passive. It makes us active—moving us closer to God and conforming us more and more to the image of Christ. When we truly believe God, our light should be shining before men, and people should be able to recognize that we are followers of Christ *because of our works*. Jesus said, "Let your light shine before men in such a way that they may see your good works, and glorify your Father who is in heaven" (Matt. 5:16). Again, we are not saved by our works, but we should be known by them, and those works should point people to the Father.

Father God, Your Word declares that I am saved by grace through faith in You, but I pray that my faith will be active, that it will spur me to demonstrate Your love and shine Your light in an empty and lost world. I pray that it will cause me to be a faithful witness for You. I am saved by grace, but let my light so shine before men that they see my good works for You.

Don't Hold Back

Ho! Every one who thirsts, come to the waters;
and you who have no money come, buy and eat.
Come, buy wine and milk without money and
without cost. Why do you spend money for what
is not bread, and your wages for what does not
satisfy? Listen carefully to Me, and eat what is
good, and delight yourself in abundance.

—ISAIAH 55:1–2

WHAT ARE YOU working for? How much of your
energy, your time, and your resources is being
given over to things that will not last? The older I
get, the more I see how quickly everything changes.
Beauty fades; money situations change; health condi-
tions change; jobs change. Everything based on circumstances is always changing. In fact anytime people
find their peace or sense of identity in something cir-
cumstantial, they are setting themselves up for a fall
because circumstances never stay the same.

This is why the Lord asks in Isaiah 55:2, "Why do you
spend money for what is not bread, and your wages for

what does not satisfy?" Beloved, don't give yourself over to things that do not last. The Bible says heaven and earth will pass away, but God's Word will never pass away (Matt. 24:35). I want to encourage you to be sold out completely to God. Don't hold anything back from Him. Give Him your time, talent, and treasure. Give your life entirely over to Him.

Jesus said, "Strive to enter through the narrow door; for many, I tell you, will seek to enter and will not be able" (Luke 13:24). Here Jesus is commanding us to call out to Him while we can, because at the end of the day, everything but Him is fleeting and temporary.

Don't hold back. "Eat what is good." Seek God with your whole heart, and you will delight yourself in abundance.

> *Father God, help me not to hold back but to give You my whole heart. Give me a desire for You that exceeds temporary satisfaction or accomplishments. By Your grace may I find delight in Your abundance.*

Pray for the Salvation of the Jewish People

For Zion's sake I will not keep silent, and for Jerusalem's sake I will not keep quiet, until her righteousness goes forth like brightness, and her salvation like a torch that is burning.

—ISAIAH 62:1

TIED UP IN God's climactic plan of redemption is the salvation of the Jewish people. That's really what Isaiah was speaking of in Isaiah 62:1. He was saying, "I'm not going to keep silent until salvation fully comes to Israel." Because the salvation of the Jewish people is so close to the heart of God, it should be close to ours as well.

Paul said he magnified his ministry to the Gentiles because through the Gentiles the Jewish people would be saved. (See Romans 11:11–14.) God is counting on the church to pray for the salvation of the Jewish people. I am thankful that our ministry is seeing Jewish salvations in Jerusalem. But there is more to be done.

When the church sends out missionaries to the nations of the world, too often the Jewish people are neglected. This should not be. The church needs to focus on the salvation of Jewish people.

Fortunately I have noticed a shift taking place as Yeshua prepares the earth for His return. People in the church are starting to realize that Jesus' return is tied up with the salvation of the Jewish people, and because of that, laborers are being sent into the harvest field in Israel. In fact *Discovering the Jewish Jesus* is broadcasting into almost every home with a television set in Israel on multiple channels, and we are sharing the good news of Messiah Yeshua with God's people in the Holy Land. But this is just the small beginnings of what the Holy Spirit wants to do.

Beloved, I encourage you to get in agreement with God. Let's go "to the Jew first, and also to the Gentile," just as the Scriptures teach. (See Romans 1:15–17; 2:9–10.)

> *Father God, I pray now that the Jewish people will be awakened to the truth that Jesus is the promised Messiah. I pray, Lord, that the eyes of their understanding would be enlightened and that they would come to know the depth of Your love for them and embrace You as their Savior and Messiah.*

Follow the Ancient Path

Thus says the LORD, "Stand by the ways and see and ask for the ancient paths, where the good way is, and walk in it; and you will find rest for your souls."

—JEREMIAH 6:16

MANY PEOPLE TODAY have thrown out everything that is traditional, but the Bible says to look for the ancient path, for the good way, and to walk in it. Obviously, as times change, we need to adapt some of our methods, but good, old-fashioned godly principles—the ancient paths of God revealed to us in Scripture—never change.

The Lord is telling us in Jeremiah 6:16 that if we are looking for wisdom, we must return to the ancient path. Return to the moral absolutes found in God's Word. Many people today create their own definition of *truth*. They follow their emotions and do what feels right. Jesus said in John 14:6, "I am the way, and the truth, and the life; no one comes to the Father but through Me." But the religion of political correctness that pervades our society today believes there must be many paths to God because there are so many religions in the world that are followed by good, decent people. And so many have thrown out the Scriptures. They have forsaken the ancient path to follow their feelings and the course of political correctness.

I want to encourage you, beloved, to seek wisdom in the ancient path. Where is the ancient path? It is written in the Hebrew Scriptures and in the New Testament. No matter what society says or how the world's morals change or even what our emotions say, we have to stick with the Word of God because it is truth (John 17:17).

Father God, Your Word is truth. I choose to believe what You have said. Help me not to be led by my emotions or the current trends of the day. Strengthen me so I do not let society dictate what I believe. Help me to trust Your Word and obey You.

Don't Waste Your Wilderness

It came about as Aaron spoke to the whole congregation of the sons of Israel, that they looked
toward the wilderness, and behold, the glory of
the LORD appeared in the cloud.

—EXODUS 16:10

GOD PREPARED THE Israelites to enter the Promised Land by having them spend forty years in
the wilderness. It may not have been the most pleasant
training ground, but it was their place of preparation
nonetheless.

In the wilderness they learned to rely on God as their
provider. In the wilderness they literally saw God's
glory revealed in a cloud by day and a pillar of fire by
night. And it was in the wilderness that the Israelites
were transformed. The God of Abraham, Isaac, and
Jacob became the God of Israel during that season as
they saw His mighty hand move on their behalf.

Beloved, I want to encourage you to look to the Lord
during wilderness experiences in your life because
there are things He teaches us and does for us in the

wilderness that He can't do when life is easier. Paul went through the wilderness of having what he called "a thorn in the flesh" (2 Cor. 12:7). We don't know exactly what this thorn in the flesh was—only that it was difficult to bear. Three times he asked God to remove it, but God's response was, "No, My power will be perfected in your weakness." (See 2 Corinthians 12:9.)

God is using your wilderness season to bring about His purpose in your life, so don't waste your wilderness. Give thanks to the Lord today for the place you find yourself in, knowing that He is using this season to bring you into a bright future.

> *Father God, thank You for having a plan for the difficult seasons in my life. I know You are using them to reveal Yourself to me in a deeper way and prepare me for what You have next for me. I trust You to use wilderness seasons in my life to make me stronger and to bring me into a deeper relationship with You.*

Bring It Into the Light

Therefore, confess your sins to one another, and pray for one another so that you may be healed. The effective prayer of a righteous man can accomplish much.

—JAMES 5:16

OVER THE YEARS, many theologians haven't known what to do with the Book of James. In fact Martin Luther the Reformer didn't think James should even be included in the Bible because he thought it emphasized works. James says, "Show me your faith without your works, and I will show you my faith by my works" (2:18, NKJV). Some theologians didn't know how to deal with James' emphasis because they were teaching salvation is by grace through faith alone. It is true: salvation is by grace through faith, but true faith produces action, obedience, and works.

Perhaps the hardest instruction James gives us to obey is the command to confess our sins one to another that we might be healed. A lot of times people keep all their sins to themselves. They have a face they put forward to the world, but they don't let anyone know who they really are. The problem with living in isolation like that, beloved, is that it keeps us in darkness and keeps us trapped. Cockroaches are free to roam as long as they are in the dark. But as soon as the light is turned on, they scramble. This is how sin and demonic oppression are. When they are in darkness, they are free to do as they please, but when sin and demonic activity are exposed to the light, they cannot continue.

This is why Jesus said through James that if you confess your sins one to another, you will be healed. Just by bringing secrets to the surface and sharing them with someone who can pray with you about them, the cleansing process begins. Through transparency, you and I are healed and made whole. Now, we need to use discretion in whom we share our lives with, but God wants you to be authentic. He wants you to have someone in your life with whom you can be honest so anything the enemy wants you to keep hidden can be brought into the light, and you can be healed.

> *Father, I ask that You show me someone I can be transparent with, someone who will pray with me that I may be healed of the things I haven't wanted to bring out into the open. Expose anything that is unlike You. Turn on the light so I can live authentically and in freedom.*

It Doesn't All Depend on God

I, the LORD, search the heart, I test the mind, even to give to each man according to his ways, according to the results of his deeds.

—JEREMIAH 17:10

THE LORD SAYS His eyes are roaming to and fro across the earth looking for somebody who will love Him (2 Chron. 16:9). You see, there is a paradox, a tension. On the one hand, God is sovereign. He does what He will with the host of heaven and the inhabitants of the earth, and He chooses individuals to bear fruit for His kingdom. Yet God gives us free will. He did not make us robots, because He wants us to choose to love Him.

Here in Jeremiah 17:10 the Lord is saying He is looking to see how we will respond to Him because how we respond to Him determines how He responds to us. Jesus said, "He who has My commandments and keeps them is the one who loves Me; and he who loves Me will be loved by My Father, and I will love him and will disclose Myself to him" (John 14:21). God's response to us is directly connected to our response to Him.

The Lord is looking for you to choose Him—to choose to love Him and to be faithful to Him. He wants you to stay connected to Him through prayer. He wants you to cry out to Him when you are in need and obey His Word. God isn't looking for you to be perfect. He just wants you to keep reaching out to Him. As you do, God's favor is going to rest upon your life. He is going to respond to you as you respond to Him. This is why Jesus said to seek first the kingdom of God and everything else will be added unto you (Matt. 6:33).

This was a hard truth for me to accept. I wanted to think everything I experienced in life depended on God, but I had to realize that some of what God does depends on me. I want to encourage you today to accept this responsibility to be accountable to God. Love Him not in your flesh but by the power of His Spirit. As you give yourself to Him and do your best to put Him first, He is going to do something marvelous in your life.

Father God, I realize that You give to each of us according to our ways. Give me a heart that says yes to You and seeks You first. If there is anything unlike You in my heart, I ask that You expose it and root it out. I pray, Lord, that when You look at me, You find me pleasing.

DAY 77

Keep Seeking

You will seek Me and find Me when you search
for Me with all your heart.

—Jeremiah 29:13

WHEN PEOPLE THINK of seeking God, they often
think finding Him is going to be some kind of
dramatic "wow" moment. In my experience, finding
God isn't just a one-time event; it is progressive. It takes
many, many years. The Bible says even Jesus grew in
stature before both God and man. I have found that it
takes a lot of work, a lot of effort, a lot of perseverance,
and a lot of pressing on to get ahold of God.

But Jeremiah 29:13 tells us that if we seek Him, we
will find Him, so don't lose heart. Keep on pressing in.
As you spend time with God each day, you are being
changed. And you are finding Him. You may not realize
it because the process happens slowly, but if you look
back on your life, you'll see that you have more peace
today than you used to have. You have more clarity of
mind. You go through life with more victory. Why?
You are slowly finding God.

The apostle Paul said this: "Not that I have already attained, or am already perfected; but I press on, that I may lay hold of that for which Christ Jesus has also laid hold of me. Brethren, I do not count myself to have apprehended; but one thing I do, forgetting those things which are behind and reaching forward to those things which are ahead, I press toward the goal for the prize of the upward call of God in Christ Jesus" (Phil. 3:12–14, NKJV). Paul had been pursuing God for years, and yet he did not count himself to have fully apprehended, and he was still pressing toward the mark.

Laying hold of that for which Christ laid hold of you is not just a quick eureka moment. It is a life of ascending up the mountain in pursuit of God. But there is glory awaiting you that is far beyond what you can imagine. So keep on pressing in and don't stop until you've laid hold of Him completely.

> *Father God, I thank You that if I seek You, I will find You. Help me to persevere in prayer, in worship, in giving, in fellowshipping with other believers, in studying Your Word, and in obedience so that I will continue to grow in my relationship with You. I believe, Father, that as I seek You, I am becoming more like You day by day.*

Jesus Will Reign

As for me, I know that my Redeemer lives, and at
the last He will take His stand on the earth.
—Job 19:25

THE BIBLE ENDS in the Book of Revelation with Jesus
materializing in the sky and God manifesting His
glory to the whole world. God Himself is going to take
His stand on the earth. It is illogical to think the God
who created this world is going to let it go on forever
without breaking in and putting things in order. This is
where it's all going.

The Bible tells us in the Book of Revelation that time
is running short and that the heightened spiritual warfare we are experiencing on earth right now is going
to intensify. When the battle between light and darkness reaches a climax, God Himself is going to come in
and dispel the darkness. He is going to put His foot on
the ground, beginning at the Mount of Olives, and He
Himself will reign on and over the earth.

Now, we can't fathom how exactly this is going to
play out. We don't know exactly or specifically what it

is going to look like. But one thing we can be sure of: God is going to interrupt the present world system. He is going to break the powers of darkness. He is going to step into this world and into the culture. He is going to cleanse it, and He Himself is going to reign on this earth that He created for His own glory.

Beloved, it's going to happen, and it's going to happen soon. Jesus said if we serve Him now, we are going to have a place of authority with Him when He reigns on the earth. This may seem far off, but Jesus will reign sooner than any of us think. So live today for the soon return of King Jesus. Jesus' last words were, "Yes, I am coming quickly" (Rev. 22:20).

> *Father God, I declare like Job that I know my Redeemer lives and at the last You will take Your stand on the earth. Help me to live with an awareness of Your soon return.*

Storm the Gates

The thief comes only to steal and kill and destroy;
I came that they may have life, and have it
abundantly.

—JOHN 10:10

JESUS SAID HE came that we may have life and have it
abundantly. But what does that mean? What is abundant life, and what does Jesus have for us?

Abundant life encompasses many things, but when I think of abundant life, I think of peace, satisfaction, love, power, authority, more than enough, and having dominion in life. Jesus wants all these things for us, but we have to storm the gates of heaven to partake of and enter into them.

Just as Israel had to drive out the Amorites, the Hittites, and the Jebusites from the Promised Land before they could take possession of it, so too do we have to drive the enemies out of our paths to enter into the fullness of what God has for us.

This means we have to come against fear. We have to come against worry. We have to come against pride. We have to come against accusation. We have to stand up to these things, come against them, and keep affirming God's truth and His Word. And when we do, we are going to find ourselves experiencing more and more freedom and more and more of the abundant life Jesus came to give.

This is a reality. Abundant life can be ours, but we have to take it. We have to storm the gates of heaven.

> *Father God, I thank You for the victory I have in You. Help me to resist the enemy's attempts to rob me of the abundant life You died for me to have. Father God, in the name of Jesus I come against every demonic power that seeks to keep me in bondage to fear, anxiety, worry, depression, anger, pride, lust, or anything else contrary to Your purpose for me. In Yeshua's name help me to walk in the fullness of what You have for me.*

Abba Father

Jesus said to him, "I am the way, and the truth, and the life; no one comes to the Father but through Me."

—JOHN 14:6

MANY TIMES WE don't consider the fact that Jesus is bringing us into relationship with the Father. Jesus said, "No one comes to the Father but through Me." You see, Jesus is the way, but Father God is the destination.

First John 3:1 says this: "Behold what manner of love the Father has bestowed on us, that we should be called children of God!" (NKJV). And we read in Romans 8:14–16: "For all who are being led by the Spirit of God, these are sons of God. For you have not received a spirit of slavery leading to fear again, but you have received a spirit of adoption as sons by which we cry out, 'Abba! Father!' The Spirit Himself testifies with our spirit that we are children of God."

Abba is the Hebrew word for *daddy* or *father*. I believe this is how God wants us to relate to Him, as our loving

Father. Yes, God is our Creator and Redeemer, and yes, He holds all power in His hands. But He does not want your relationship with Him to be distant. He wants it to have the intimacy a loving father has with his children. So I want to encourage you to watch how you are praying. If you are only addressing Him as "God" when you pray or only praying to Jesus, begin to address God as Father. Jesus taught us to pray in this way: "Our Father who is in heaven" (Matt. 6:9).

The Father sent Jesus to bring us to Himself. Jesus is the way, but Abba is the destination.

> *Father God, You sent Jesus to bring me to You. I cry out to You right now, Abba! Daddy! I pray that You give me a deeper revelation of Your fatherly love for me.*

Step Out of the Boat

Believe Me that I am in the Father and the Father is in Me; otherwise believe because of the works themselves. Truly, truly, I say to you, he who believes in Me, the works that I do, he will do also; and greater works than these he will do; because I go to the Father.

—JOHN 14:11–12

THE SAME ANOINTING, the same Holy Spirit that was on Jesus and in Jesus, is on and in His people today. We will do the same works that Jesus did and in a greater way because the church is not made up of one person but of everyone who is born again and has received the Spirit of God. What this means is if you have the courage as a believer in Yeshua to lay hands on people and pray for them, to take authority over demonic spirits, you are going to see results.

I cannot explain why sometimes people get healed and sometimes they don't, but what I can tell you is this: if you will consistently lay your hands on those who are sick—your friends, loved ones, family, coworkers, etc.—and just say, "Jesus, I take authority over this sickness in Your name; I curse it at the root, and I speak Your healing," you will see results. You can take authority over cancer, you can take authority over demonic spirits, and you can release wholeness in Yeshua's name. Jesus went throughout Judea healing the sick and casting out devils, and He said greater works than these shall you do. But you have to step out of the boat.

Father God, I thank You that in You I have the authority to cast out demons and to pray for the sick and see them recover. I pray that You give me greater confidence in the power of Your Spirit that lives in me. Help me to walk in the fullness of Your power. Your Word says that the church will do greater works than what Jesus did while He walked the earth. I ask that You cause me to live in that reality.

He Calls Us Friends

No longer do I call you slaves, for the slave does not know what his master is doing; but I have called you friends, for all things that I have heard from My Father I have made known to you.

—John 15:15

IT IS SUCH a beautiful reality that Jesus looks at us as His friends. Think about it for a second. The Son of God Himself considers you and me His friends. It's hard to wrap our minds around this. But God's Word says that His heart is full of love for us, and He calls us His friends.

You are the friend of Jesus, and He wants you to share your heart with Him. He considers you a partner in life, someone with whom He will have communion and fellowship. This may be hard for you to believe, but Jesus actually enjoys your company, and He wants to share with you a deeper revelation of who He is and what is on His heart.

Let's take Yeshua at His word and believe that He sees us as His friends. Believe Him when He says He does not see you as a servant but instead calls you His friend.

> *You said, Jesus, that everything the Father reveals to You, You are going to reveal to me. So right now I'm coming to You, King Jesus, asking You to continue to reveal the Father's love to me and reveal all things that will build me up in the revelation of Your beauty, who You are, who the Father is, and my destiny in You. I love You today. Thank You for making me Your friend.*

Deny Yourself

For the grace of God has appeared, bringing salvation to all men, instructing us to deny ungodliness and worldly desires and to live sensibly, righteously and godly in the present age.

—TITUS 2:11–12

WHEN YESHUA APPEARED, revelation came into our hearts from heaven, and the revelation was this: we should live godly lives by denying worldly desires. But unfortunately the gospel many are hearing today is one that feeds the flesh and doesn't call on people to deny themselves.

The gospel the apostles delivered to us involves sacrifice. Yet sadly sometimes we only obey God when it is convenient. And when we are called to deny ourselves, we push away the conviction of the Holy Spirit and do what we want.

Jesus said if we are to come after Him, we must pick up our cross, deny ourselves, and follow Him. What does it mean to pick up our cross? It means we sacrifice what we want. Jesus denied what His flesh wanted.

He didn't want to go to the cross in His flesh, but He denied what He wanted to be obedient to the Father.

I don't know what the Father has been speaking to you about—where He is asking you to discipline yourself or what He is asking you to give up for Him. But, beloved, if you want to know Him in a deep way, you have to obey. And if you choose His narrow path, He will reveal more and more of Himself and His love to you. And not only that, beloved, but Jesus is coming back soon, and His reward is with Him, so stay the course and deny ungodliness.

Father God, I ask that You help me take up my cross and deny my flesh so I can live sensibly, righteously, and godly before You each day.

It's Time to Get Ready

Because you have kept the word of My perseverance, I also will keep you from the hour of testing, that hour which is about to come upon the whole world, to test those who dwell on the earth.

—REVELATION 3:10

I HAVE NEWS FOR you, beloved. Life is going to get harder. But Jesus said in Revelation 3:10 that if we live for Him completely now, we will be able to stand as the world becomes increasingly darker and more oppressive.

The time to prepare for difficulty is not when it comes. You have to get ready for hardship beforehand. Our military personnel don't prepare for battle when they're in the midst of the fighting. They train in advance so when the conflict comes, they will be able to stand.

I can promise you this: we are not headed for a utopia. There will not be lasting peace on earth until Messiah Yeshua comes and reigns over the world. Until then the world is going to get worse.

Paul said in 2 Timothy 3:1 that "in the last days difficult times will come." Jesus said, "At that time many will fall away and will betray one another and hate one another. Many false prophets will arise and will mislead many. Because lawlessness is increased, most people's love will grow cold....For then there will be a great tribulation, such as has not occurred since the beginning of the world until now, nor ever will" (Matt. 24:10–12, 21).

Right now the Holy Spirit is restraining the enemy and the chaos he wants to unleash in the world. But as we get closer to Messiah's return, the Holy Spirit will begin to draw back, and then pandemonium will arise.

Now is the time to get ready. We need to practice loving the Lord with all our heart, soul, mind, and strength today, not tomorrow. Jesus promised that if we practice putting Him first today, when things get difficult, we will overcome. In fact light shines even brighter in the darkness.

Yeshua is coming soon, but until He does, we will see more and more chaos and hardship arising in the world. We are not to fear. But we must be serious and get prepared while we still can.

> *Father God, I know that in this world there will be tribulation, but Your Word declares that You have overcome the world. Lord, help me not to fear suffering but to live confidently as I look forward and prepare myself for Your return. Strengthen me by Your grace so that I will be faithful to You until the end.*

DAY 85

God Rejoices Over You

The LORD your God is in your midst, a victorious warrior. He will exult over you with joy, He will be quiet in His love, He will rejoice over you with shouts of joy.

—ZEPHANIAH 3:17

I THINK IT CAN be hard for us as human beings who face tragedies and hardships to truly grasp how much God loves us. I know it is for me. We're faced with so many challenges in this world. We see so much suffering around us, so many people in pain, so much divorce, so many people who have been betrayed in relationships. We are surrounded by darkness, and when we live in this world for long, we can become jaded by it.

Then we read a verse like Zephaniah 3:17 that tells us the Lord loves us so much He is shouting over us. His banner over us is love (Song of Sol. 2:4). To believe God loves us with such abandon truly requires a paradigm shift that takes our eyes off the spiritual darkness we encounter in this world and onto the pure light of God's supernatural love for us.

Beloved, I want to tell you today that above the clouds of this world is the Son of God, whose love is beaming down on our lives. In fact Father God loves you with the same strength with which He loves Jesus Himself. You see, all of the Father's love is focused on His Son, and you and I have been adopted into and are now in the Son. (See Ephesians 1:5.)

Whatever pressures you are facing, it is going to be OK. You are going to make it to the end, and there awaits you a crown of righteousness and heaven itself. (See 2 Timothy 4:8.) Darkness lasts for a night, but joy comes in the morning.

God loves you, beloved. No matter what you have done or how you have missed the mark, God rejoices over you with shouts of joy. Believe it!

Father God, it is amazing to me that You would rejoice over me with shouts of joy, but I believe Your Word. Thank You for loving me so extravagantly and for raising a banner of victory over my life. I believe I am more than a conqueror in You.

Be Bold for Jesus

What I tell you in the darkness, speak in the light; and what you hear whispered in your ear, proclaim upon the housetops.

—MATTHEW 10:27

FRIENDS, THERE IS no such thing as a secret Christian. There is no such thing as a believer who never shares his faith. When Jesus was on this earth, one of the last instructions He gave was for us to "go into all the world and preach the gospel to all creation" (Mark 16:15). That is the Great Commission, and it is for everyone.

You and I have an assignment on the earth to be bold witnesses for Jesus. We are called to extend and expand the kingdom of God. Jesus said in today's verse that we are to shout from the rooftops whatever He whispers in our ears. The apostle Paul said in 2 Corinthians 5:20 that we are Christ's ambassadors, entreating the world to be reconciled to God. And Jesus said in Matthew 5:13–14 that we are the salt of the earth and the light of the world, so we ought to let our light shine. In these passages and others God has made His will for us clear.

So I want to encourage you: don't be timid. God has not given you a spirit of fear (2 Tim. 1:7), so be a bold witness for Him. Jesus said, "Whoever is ashamed of Me and My words, the Son of Man will be ashamed of him when He comes in His glory" (Luke 9:26). Beloved, we can't keep quiet. We need to speak of Jesus to those we are in relationship with here on earth. We need to talk about Jesus at the grocery store, at the salon, at the gym. Wherever we go, Jesus should be on our lips. We should be His fragrance in the world.

Yes, we need wisdom in how to approach people, but we can't be stalled by fear and analysis paralysis. We should always be directing people to God, even in small ways. When someone asks how you're doing, you can say, "I'm doing well, praise God!" Or you can simply offer to pray for someone and remind him that Jesus loves him. Directing people to Jesus is our assignment on the earth. Let's love God by doing what He instructed us to do.

> *Father God, You have called me to be a bold witness for You. Help me to never shrink back from my assignment. Father, I ask that You give me divine opportunities to tell those I come in contact with about You. Show me how to make witnessing for You a natural part of my lifestyle.*

The Counsel of the Holy Spirit

The counsel of the LORD is with those who fear Him, and He will make His covenant known to them.

—PSALM 25:14, MEV

S O MANY TIMES when I've needed direction, God has spoken to me supernaturally. Whether it was a slow, emerging awareness of what I should do; a sudden burst of supernatural anointing that brought insight; or a dream in the night, the Lord spoke to me with the spirit of counsel. I know this is why I have come so far since I accepted Yeshua as Messiah—because I have been upheld, consoled, and directed by the counsel of the Holy Spirit.

I want to encourage you to believe that God will personally counsel you. Oftentimes God's people are not receiving the fullness of the counsel the Father has for them because rather than looking to the Father, they are looking, first and almost exclusively, to their friends for counsel. In other words, when faced with a problem, rather than looking to God about the issue, rather than praying about it, rather than expecting Father God to answer and direct us, they go out and tell all their friends, looking to them for solutions.

Please do not misunderstand me. There is wisdom in talking to people, and I have confidants in my life whom I seek for insight. After all the Bible says that "in the multitude of counselors there is safety" (Prov. 11:14, NKJV). But we must remember to look first and foremost to the Lord for wisdom.

Those who fear the Lord are going to receive the counsel of the Holy Spirit. It is part of His ministry to you. God wants to direct your path. Jesus said, "If you abide in Me, you will bear much fruit." (See John 15:4–5.) So, beloved, direct your heart back to relying on Jesus for everything. God is in the here and the now, His counsel is practical, and He will make it known to those who seek Him.

> *Holy Spirit, thank You for being my Counselor. I know You use many resources to communicate with us, but help me to look to You first for wisdom, and strengthen me to wait for Your answer.*

He Helps Us Carry Our Burdens

Blessed be the Lord, who daily bears our burden,
the God who is our salvation. Selah.

—PSALM 68:19

DO YOU REALIZE that every single day God is helping you carry your burdens? Have you ever started a day worried and agitated, then cried out to God, and a few hours later you realized the anxiety had lifted and you had peace in your heart? That happened because God was bearing your burden. Through Jesus, Father God was imparting His strength to you.

Beloved one, Jesus really does help you bear your burdens. That is why He said, "Come to Me, all who are weary and heavy-laden, and I will give you rest" (Matt. 11:28). If you are facing a difficult time in your marriage, with your finances, on your job, or in your family, remember that you are not alone. Jesus wants to help you bear those burdens.

For the rest of your life God will be with you, no

matter what you face. Nothing will be too much for you because the One who rose from the grave lives inside you. He will help you bear your burdens and make you more than a conqueror all the days of your life.

Father God, I just want to say thank You for helping me bear my burdens. So many times I've had days when I started out so agitated, but I cried out to You, and before the day ended, You gave me peace and strength. That anxiety was just loosed somehow. So, Father, I want to say thank You and acknowledge that it was because of You. Father, thank You for always being there.

The Gift of Conviction

Search me, O God, and know my heart; try me and know my anxious thoughts; and see if there be any hurtful way in me, and lead me in the everlasting way.

—PSALM 139:23–24

IN THIS PSALM David was praying for the conviction of the Holy Spirit. That may seem like a strange thing to pray for, but hear me: the conviction of the Holy Spirit is a gift.

David asked God to search his heart and show him if there was any wrong way in him and then cleanse him of anything that wasn't of God. Conviction is a gift because when we open our hearts to let the Holy Spirit tell us the truth about ourselves and then choose to agree with what He says, He cleanses and transforms us.

The Bible says, "If we confess our sins, He is faithful and righteous to forgive us our sins and to cleanse us from all unrighteousness" (1 John 1:9). So when the Holy Spirit shows us something about our heart or our thinking that is wrong, and we say, "Yes, Father God, save me, forgive me, wash me, cleanse me," that conviction becomes the agent of the Holy Spirit to supernaturally wash us of that thing so we can be free from it.

I love the discipline of the Father. I am so thankful that He corrects us. I want to encourage you not to be afraid of the conviction of the Holy Spirit. Be like David, who asked God to show him if there was anything wrong in the way he was thinking or feeling or the motives of his heart. Be an open book to God so He can cleanse you and bring you into deep fellowship with Himself.

Beloved, Jesus loves you. Submit to His process of sanctification.

> *Thank You, Father God, for the gift of conviction. I pray like David that You will search my heart, O God, "and know my anxious thoughts; and see if there be any hurtful way in me, and lead me in the everlasting way." Cleanse me of anything that displeases You.*

Stake Your Faith on God's Word

When He approached Jerusalem, He saw the city and wept over it, saying, "If you had known in this day, even you, the things which make for peace! But now they have been hidden from your eyes. For the days will come upon you when your enemies will throw up a barricade against you, and surround you and hem you in on every side, and they will level you to the ground and your children within you, and they will not leave in you one stone upon another, because you did not recognize the time of your visitation."

—LUKE 19:41–44

NO MATTER THEIR religious background, tourists in Jerusalem often visit the Western Wall, which is the retaining wall that held up the Temple Mount.

In Luke 19, when Jesus approached Jerusalem, He wept over the city and prophesied the words in verses 41–44. Yeshua foretold the destruction of the temple, and today all that is left is the retaining wall. The point is that approximately forty years after Yeshua prophesied the destruction of the second temple, His words came to pass when the Romans came in and destroyed the temple in AD 70. We need to take Yeshua's words seriously. Every prophecy Jesus spoke has either been fulfilled or will be fulfilled. Let's continue to stake our faith on the Word of God. It never returns void.

Stop and consider how much things have changed in the world today. Think about how different the moral standards were when you were younger as opposed to what is morally acceptable today. The point is everything around us is changing, and we have to make a decision as to whether we will yield to the ever-changing spirit of the age or we will stake and root our souls in the unchanging Word of God.

> *Father God, Your Word is living and active; it is sharper than any two-edged sword, dividing even soul from spirit and joint from marrow and judging the thoughts and attitudes of the heart. Father, Your Word is a lamp unto my feet and a light unto my path. I trust Your Word and stake my faith on its truth. I know all of its promises are yes in Messiah Jesus and amen, and it will never return void. Your Word is life, and I declare that every word You have spoken over my life will be fulfilled.*

Close the Door to Fear

In God, whose word I praise, in God I have put my trust; I shall not be afraid. What can mere man do to me?

—Psalm 56:4

I BELIEVE THE MOST common problem known to man is fear. Everyone wars against it in some shape or form. A lot of times people say the opposite of love is hate, but oftentimes beneath hate is fear.

The Lord said not to fear over a hundred times in the Bible. So I want to encourage you today to stand against fear. The psalmist stood up to fear, saying he would not be afraid because he put his trust in God. Beloved, we too must decide to close our hearts to fear. God is calling us to reject fear and refuse to let it in.

Just as the Lord spoke to Joshua, He is telling us, "Have I not commanded you? Be strong and courageous! Do not tremble or be dismayed, for the LORD your God is with you wherever you go" (Josh. 1:9).

Fear is a thief. It will steal your peace, your confidence, and your hope for the future. So you have to come against fear before it gets in. As soon as you begin to sense fear, the minute it begins to knock, that's when you need to say, "No!"

And if fear is already taking up space in your heart, stand up against those fears and begin to close the door to them by agreeing with God. God has said He doesn't want fear to have a place in your life. He has said, "I am your friend. I have you in the palm of My hand. Do not be afraid." (See Isaiah 41:10.) So make a decision to agree with love, to agree with God, to agree with His Word. God doesn't want you to be afraid. He loves you, He's protecting you, and He's going to take care of you. Remind yourself of that truth as often as you need to, and keep fear out.

Father God, Your Word says You have not given me a spirit of fear but a spirit of power and of love and a sound mind. I choose to agree with Your Word rather than giving in to fear. I trust that You have me in the palm of Your hand, and I will never be forsaken. I rebuke fear right now and command it to leave in the name of Messiah Jesus. Father, may my mind and heart be filled with Your peace and Your perfect love that casts out fear. In Jesus' name, amen.

DAY 92

You Are Being Changed

But we all, with unveiled face, beholding as in a mirror the glory of the Lord, are being transformed into the same image from glory to glory, just as from the Lord, the Spirit.

—2 Corinthians 3:18

THIS VERSE IS one of my favorites in the entire Bible. It is telling us that as we focus on the Lord and His Word, we are seeing into the Spirit of Jesus Himself. And as we look upon Jesus, the Spirit of the Lord is supernaturally transforming us into His image. We are going from glory to glory and from strength to strength. Simply put, you and I are being changed.

This is one of the greatest miracles you can ever experience—to look at your life and see how Jesus has changed you. When you think about what you were like five years ago, you should notice that you are different. You should see that you have changed because everything that is alive is growing and changing. Only something that is dead remains the same. Of all the miracles I have experienced in my life, seeing how God is changing me is one of the most thrilling.

We are being changed even into the image of Jesus Himself. So I speak transformation over your life right now by the power of the Spirit of the living God. I want to encourage you, beloved one, to know that as you seek first the kingdom of God and make Jesus first in your life, He is going to do amazing things in your life. He is going to do more than you can ask or think. He is changing you, and you are going to be doubly blessed.

Father God, I thank You that I am not the same as I was last year or even last month. As I look to You and yield to Your Word, I am becoming more like You. I thank You for moving me from glory to glory and from strength to strength and transforming me in the process.

Trust His Love

And the Scripture was fulfilled which says, "And Abraham believed God, and it was reckoned to him as righteousness," and he was called the friend of God.

—James 2:23

THIS VERSE REFERENCES God's words in Genesis 15:6, but they do not apply only to Abraham.

Still today, believing God—believing He loves you and will do what He says He's going to do—will bring you into right standing with your Creator. That's what righteousness is—to be in a right relationship with HaShem, the Lord our Creator. And when we are in a right relationship with God, we can trust what Father God tells us. We believe He is good and that He is going to work all things together for our good. We believe He is in control and that we are not just subject to all types of randomness and chaos in this world but that God is reigning over our lives. When we truly believe God on that level and open our hearts to Him, we will experience friendship with Him.

When you think about it, can you really be in close relationship with someone you don't trust, someone whose word you don't believe? To be close with anyone, you must be able to believe that person is who he claims to be and that he will keep his promises to you. That is why God longs for us to trust that He loves us and will never leave us nor forsake us. He knows that if we can't believe Him, we can't experience the level of intimacy He wants to have with us. We receive what we believe in.

We must get hold of the depth of God's love for us. And as we do, we're going to experience more and more joy, peace, freedom, and power. God loves you. He has taken your sin out of the way through Jesus' sacrifice. All that's left, beloved, is for you, by the power of the Holy Spirit, to open your heart to Him and trust Him and His love for you.

> *Father God, thank You for loving me. Thank You for having a good plan for me, a plan to prosper me and not to harm me, a plan to give me hope and a future. Father God, I ask that You help me to receive the great love You have for me. I ask that You expose any area where I struggle to believe You. Help me to trust You.*

Set Apart

Paul, a bond-servant of Christ Jesus, called as an apostle, set apart for the gospel of God.

—ROMANS 1:1

PAUL SAID HE was "called as an apostle, set apart for the gospel of God." But guess what? In a sense so are you. We all have been set apart for the gospel of God.

We are holy because Christ has made us holy, and the word *holy* means set apart. If God has set us apart for Himself, we need to live in a way that reflects that fact. (See 1 Peter 1:15–21.) We should not look or act like the world because we have come out of the world. We have been chosen to be salt and light. (See Matthew 5:13–14.) We are in the world but not of the world.

You are special because God chose you out of the world and set you apart. Jesus said, "You did not choose Me but I chose you, and appointed you that you would go and bear fruit, and that your fruit would remain" (John 15:16). That is true of all God's children. And why did God set you apart? It was for the gospel. God wants you and me to touch people with the good news of Jesus.

Once I went to a restaurant that I had not visited in a long time. After I was seated, the waitress came to my table and said she remembered me from when I was there previously. The woman looked vaguely familiar, but I didn't remember her well. She remembered me because I told her about Jesus and prayed with her. That prayer opened her heart so much that during my subsequent visit, she pulled a chair up to my table and asked if I would pray for her because the restaurant was closing and she didn't know what she was going to do.

It may not always seem like it, but people are hungry for the good news. People are lost and hurting and in darkness. When you reach out to them in love and tell them Jesus loves them or ask to pray for them, you don't know how much that will often mean to them.

So, beloved, let's be who Jesus has called us to be. We are set apart unto God to show His love by sharing the good news of His kingdom with the world.

> *Father God, thank You for choosing me out of the world and setting me apart for You. Help me to be a light in this world, revealing Your love and truth to those who are in need and hurting. I thank You, Father, for giving me opportunities to touch people with the good news of the gospel. Help me to make the most of each chance I have to be a witness for You.*

DAY 95

Depend on the Holy Spirit

> For I know that nothing good dwells in me, that is, in my flesh; for the willing is present in me, but the doing of the good is not.... Wretched man that I am! Who will set me free from the body of this death? Thanks be to God through Jesus Christ our Lord!
>
> —ROMANS 7:18, 24–25

THESE WORDS FROM the apostle Paul are as true for you and me as they were for him. Nothing good dwells in our flesh, but we have victory through Messiah Jesus. How do we experience this victory? Only by depending on the Holy Spirit. We cannot overcome in our flesh.

Beloved, no matter how much we want to, we don't have the power to do good without the enabling of the Holy Spirit. We are all created in the image of God, and because of this we see certain attributes in all human beings. Take, for example, the ability to show kindness. Even mothers who don't know the Lord are, generally speaking, kind and loving to their children. This shows that because we are created in God's image, certain parts of our nature reflect His goodness. But at the end of the day, humanity is in bondage to sin and separated from the life of the Spirit.

To transcend this spiritual darkness and enter into victory, we must live a life of dependency on the Holy Spirit. Only by following His leading will we be able to resist the desires of our flesh. Sometimes God sends trials because He wants to break us down so we will become wholly dependent on Him.

> *Father God, thank You for destining me to triumph in Messiah Yeshua. I know that no good thing dwells in my flesh, but as I depend on Your Spirit, You will lead me to victory. Help me to walk by Your Spirit.*

Because of His Righteousness

> But now apart from the Law the righteousness of God has been manifested, being witnessed by the Law and the Prophets, even the righteousness of God through faith in Jesus Christ for all those who believe; for there is no distinction.
>
> —ROMANS 3:21–22

OF ALL THE truths in Scripture, this is one of the most fundamental: your righteousness before God is apart from the works of the law. This is because the righteousness we enter into when we accept Yeshua as Savior is not based on our perfect obedience to the law, as in the Mosaic covenant, but rather on the righteousness of Jesus.

When Paul says the righteousness of God has been revealed from heaven apart from the works of the law, he means that God has shown His righteousness by keeping the covenant He made with Abraham, Isaac, and Jacob to send a Redeemer. You see, God told Abraham that through his seed, all the nations of the earth would be blessed (Gen. 22:18). This blessing comes through Yeshua Messiah, who becomes the righteousness of all who believe.

So, beloved, don't confuse your faith in Jesus with your works. We live holy lives because we love Him and want to walk blameless before Him, not because we are trying to earn His love or favor. God loves you unconditionally, and your righteousness is based solely on the righteousness of Messiah Yeshua, not on your works. So take confidence in the fact that because you are in Yeshua, you are God's righteousness.

> *Lord Jesus, it is because of Your righteousness that I am saved. I couldn't have been good enough to ever earn Your love. Thank You for giving Your love freely and dying on the cross so I could spend eternity with You. Help me to love You with my life by walking in obedience and living in the light of Your truth.*

The Beginning and End of Our Faith

I will put My Spirit within you and cause you to walk in My statutes, and you will be careful to observe My ordinances.

—Ezekiel 36:27

ALTHOUGH EZEKIEL WAS an Old Testament prophet, this verse is speaking of a new covenant reality. God is saying that in the new covenant, which was fulfilled in Messiah Jesus, God would cause us to walk in His ways.

God is at work in me and in you "both to will and to do for His good pleasure" (Phil. 2:13, NKJV). This means that God's Spirit is moving in our lives, imparting His divine nature to us so we develop a natural affinity to love what God loves and to do what He does. In other words, He is causing us to walk in the ways of His Spirit. Our desire to please God, our passion to share the gospel, our heart to know Him on a deeper level—these are not desires we are creating ourselves; rather, God is creating them in us.

Hebrews 12:2 tells us that Jesus is the author and the finisher of our faith. Our faith began with God revealing Himself to us, drawing us to Himself, and then causing us to be born again by His Spirit. It was a supernatural work. John wrote that those who are born again "were born, not of blood nor of the will of the flesh nor of the will of man, but of God" (John 1:13). In other words, when you are born again, you are born of God's Spirit because of something supernatural that God did.

In the same way God caused you to be born again through nothing you did or produced, He is continually imparting His nature to you. That nature goes to work in your life and transforms you, and progressively you find yourself walking in God's ways because of His divine activity in your life.

Beloved, God is the awesome beginning and end of your faith. You can trust Him who is faithful to complete in you what He began.

> *Father God, thank You for putting Your Spirit within me and causing me to walk in Your ways. I thank You that my righteousness does not depend on me and that You even work in me a desire to do Your will. Thank You, Father, for making me a partaker of Your divine nature and transforming me by the power of Your Spirit.*

Forever Settled

But God demonstrates His own love toward us, in that while we were yet sinners, Christ died for us.

—ROMANS 5:8

ONCE WHEN I was ministering at a congregation in Toledo, Ohio, I asked the people to raise their hand if they sometimes wonder whether God really loves them. I would say roughly half the congregation raised their hand in response to my question. But I wasn't really surprised. I have felt that way myself.

Despite hearing that God loves us and knowing it is repeatedly declared in Scripture, sometimes we wake up and just don't feel God's love. For whatever reason, some days we try to reach out to God, and we just don't feel connected to Him. But over the years I have learned what I must do when I begin to feel that way—I have to turn to and focus on the truth of God's Word.

The Bible says in Romans 5:8 that God proved His love for us by sending Jesus to die for us when we weren't even looking for Him. It says that while we were yet sinners, Messiah died for us. We don't have to wonder if God loves us because that verse answers the question. Yes, beloved, God loves us, and He proved it in objective reality when Jesus went to the cross.

So on those days when you are not feeling emotionally connected to God, remember the Word. God loves you. That fact is forever settled. He loved you before you even knew who He was. Remind yourself of that whenever you don't "feel" anything. Faith isn't based on feeling. It is based on the Word of God, and the Word says God really loves you. Let's believe even when we don't feel it.

> *Father God, thank You for loving me even when I don't feel anything. Help me to live in the reality of this truth.*

Strike the Rock

"Behold, I will stand before you there on the rock at Horeb; and you shall strike the rock, and water will come out of it, that the people may drink." And Moses did so in the sight of the elders of Israel.

—Exodus 17:6

IN EXODUS 17 the children of Israel were wandering in the wilderness and couldn't find water, so they began to grumble and complain. Moses cried out to God, asking Him what to do, and the Lord told Moses to strike the rock and water would come out. Moses did as the Lord said, and God supernaturally provided water for the people to drink.

There are many lessons to glean from this miracle, but I want to point out something simple but, I believe, quite profound. God intervened supernaturally, but Moses had a part to play. The Lord could have just spoken to the rock and caused water to flow out of it, but instead He had Moses do something. He told him to strike the rock to bring the water forth. The same thing happened when the Israelites were at the Red Sea with the Egyptians in hot pursuit. The Lord had Moses do something—stretch out his staff over the sea—before He parted the water.

The same thing is happening in your life and in mine. It is as we are obeying the Lord, as we are moving forward in life, as we are following His voice, that miracles happen. If you are obedient to the Lord, you will find that supernatural blessings will follow you, just as they followed Moses.

> *Father God, You are still a supernatural, miracle-working God who intervenes in the lives of Your people. I choose to strike the rock—to walk in obedience to Your Word—and as I do, I believe I will see miracles and breakthrough in my life. Thank You in advance for manifesting Your supernatural power to me and giving me victory.*

Focus on Things Eternal

Therefore, prepare your minds for action, keep sober in spirit, fix your hope completely on the grace to be brought to you at the revelation of Jesus Christ.

—1 PETER 1:13

IN THE CHURCH world today we are not often challenged to be looking for Jesus' return. That combined with the fact that He hasn't yet come in ages past has caused many Christians to stop looking for His appearing altogether.

But Peter is saying that we should completely fix our minds on the fact that Jesus is coming back and will reward us for what we have done in this life. We see this truth throughout Scripture. Jesus' last words in the last chapter of the last book of the New Testament are "Yes, I am coming quickly" (Rev. 22:20). He has also promised to reward us for everything we do for Him while on this earth waiting for Him. Yeshua said, "Behold, I am coming quickly, and My reward is with Me, to render to every man according to what he has done" (Rev. 22:12).

Not a cup of cold water given in His name will go unrewarded (Matt. 10:42).

Beloved, focus on more than temporary satisfactions. Set your focus on things that are eternal, because Messiah Jesus is coming back soon, and He is coming back for you!

> *Father God, help me to focus on eternal things and to always keep in mind that Messiah Jesus is coming back for those who know Him. Help me to keep focusing on the joy set before me and what I must do while I am on this earth. Help me to never lose sight of the fact that I must tell others about You because You are coming back soon.*

About the Author

MESSIANIC RABBI KIRT A. Schneider, a Jewish believer in Jesus and end-times messenger of the Lord, delivers the word of the Lord with a true passion of the Holy Spirit. When Rabbi Schneider was twenty years old, the Lord suddenly awakened him and revealed Himself as Jesus the Messiah on the cross, and his life has never been the same. He has since pastored, traveled internationally as an evangelist, and served as rabbi of a Messianic synagogue.

Rabbi Schneider is the host of the international television broadcast *Discovering the Jewish Jesus*, which can be seen seven days a week in more than one hundred million homes in the United States and approximately two hundred nations worldwide. Viewers tune in regularly as Rabbi Schneider shows with exceptional clarity how the Old and New Testaments connect and how Jesus completes the unfolding plan of God. For a list of times and stations that broadcast Rabbi Schneider's program in your area, visit www.DiscoveringTheJewishJesus.com and click on the "Ways to Watch" tab.

In addition to hosting mass evangelistic crusades and broadcasting through television all around the world, Rabbi Schneider is the author of five books, including *Lion of Judah*, *Experiencing the Supernatural*, *The Book of Revelation Decoded*, and *Awakening to Messiah*. He and his wife, Cynthia, have two children.

www.DiscoveringTheJewishJesus.com